BREAKING THE MYTH OF LEADERSHIP: THE SOLUTION TO AFRICA'S CRISIS

BREAKING THE MYTH OF LEADERSHIP: THE SOLUTION TO AFRICA'S CRISIS

Nana Osei-Bonsu Jr

ISBN-13: 9781976377235
ISBN-10: 1976377234

To my wonderful parents, Mr. Charles Kwame Adjei Osei-Bonsu—you gave us the greatest gift of life we could ever dream of, and your profound wisdom and dedication to life as well as your weaknesses have made us all better people in life. And to Mrs. Christiana Ama Asieduah—your gentle and loving soul makes you the most beautiful woman I have ever known. Your strength, your prayers, and your commitment to the values of life are what shaped us all to become who we are today. We would always choose you two to be our parents without hesitation if given the opportunity. We, as your children, love you so dearly.

To the late Dr. David Abdulai and all the unknown leaders out there, all over the world, who are selflessly in service to humanity, making sure that you fulfill your purpose to make the world a better place for generations to come. Your work is never in vain; we are experiencing the ripple effect of your love and dedication.

To the youth of Africa, as well as all the struggling youth in every part of the globe. Your pursuit of discovering your gift,

*knowledge, wisdom, and understanding will always bring you illu-
mination, which will ultimately lead you to serve your generation
with love and joy.*

Table of Contents

Imam Ali, one of the greatest and most knowledgeable figures in Islam, made great strides to ensure his governors and officials were free from corruption and greed and treated people with dignity, honor, and kindness. He told his officials, "Behave humbly with the people, keep yourself lenient, meet them with a big heart, and accord them equal treatment, so that the high should not expect injustices from you in their favor, and the low should not be despondent of your justice towards them."

This quote sums up a great deal about leadership to me. Our society has allowed so many things to pass as leadership when it ordinarily should not be so. In our parts, "leadership" has been misconstrued to mean "obedience" and "command."

Many countries in the world, including Ghana, have had periods in their history when authoritarianism and dictatorships took root and stifled society. It was either by a corrupt civilian capturing a state, aided by brute security forces, or security forces themselves seizing power. They muzzle the press, clamp down on personal liberties, and eliminate any form of institution that can hold them accountable, such as the judiciary.

As a barracks boy, I know and have experienced firsthand this concept of leadership. While it instills a great sense of discipline, it can also breed a crop of self-serving rogues, as evident in Ghana and across much of the world.

There are many countries (especially in Africa) whose systems have been built around and to serve one person's family and cronies. In fact, many of these African "leaders" genuinely believe that their countries would be in total disarray without their presence, and so they change constitutions to remove age and term limits to allow them to entrench their hold on these countries.

That may be true looking at a country such as Libya post-Gaddafi, but that also presents a good case study of how leadership should not be done, for I believe that the true essence of a leader can best be felt when he is no longer around. In the leader's absence is when his true worth is discovered.

The importance of leadership cannot be underestimated, and while I am of the firm belief that no one is born a follower, I believe leadership is the work one is born to do. One may be born with charisma and the gift of the gab, but that is not all that leadership is about.

Nana Osei-Bonsu Jr captures leadership brilliantly when he lists service, talent, selflessness, and self-fulfillment as the elements of a good leader. Leadership is nurtured and culti-vated over a long period of time.

Misconceptions about leadership have gone a long way to prevent many potential leaders from refusing to see themselves as such. While elected, political office is one track to leadership; it is certainly not the only way a person can serve society. As an investigative journalist, I serve society by bringing attention to its deficiencies so that they can be solved. Another unelected leader I know is the late Dr. David Abdulai, who during his lifetime dedicated himself to serving the ill and the poor in the north of Ghana. It is of no surprise that his great contributions have been captured beautifully in this book. And there are many other ways one can become a leader or display leadership qualities—from the pulpit or minbar of the Imams, from the classroom, or even on the field as a football player.

The likes of Dr. Abdulai did not make money because of their work, but they served humanity in tremendous ways. Many assume money and power are the rewards that come with leadership, and I believe that is one of the reasons why many African societies have not transformed as much as they should have. Many are those who enter or strive for the corridors of power in a bid to enrich themselves and their families.

Corruption has thus become a bane in our quest for good leadership, and it is incumbent on all of us to ensure that it does not take hold of our society. While bad leaders are a reflection of the society in which they live, I refuse to believe that Africa has no transformational and impactful leaders—those leaders have simply not discovered their potentials yet.

In this book, Nana Osei-Bonsu Jr has tried to challenge our conceptions of what leadership is and what it ought to be. He challenges all of us to identify our purpose in life and the things that drive us and to take up positions of leadership to serve not just ourselves or the present but to leave a lasting legacy for generations unborn, and it is my firm hope that all who read this book take up that challenge.

I would like to end this foreword with a quote by Mahatma Gandhi, and I hope it inspires all of us to do our bit to see our continent go in the direction that it ought to.

"Be the change that you wish to see in the world."

—Anas Aremeyaw Anas, undercover journalist and lawyer

I want to express my heartfelt gratitude to the following people, whose inspiration and belief in me made this publication possible. First of all to my brother from another mother, Mr. Prince Ofosu-Mensah, who happens to be my biggest fan and inspiration. He has always believed in me from the very first day we met. He helped proofread the manuscript. And I can't forget his beautiful wife, Thelma Ofosu-Mensah. I hold you guys so dear to my heart.

To my wonderful friend Anas Aremeyaw Anas, an ace, world-renowned undercover journalist, and lawyer, who is an example of service leadership in our generation. He is making an impact in this and generations to come. Thank you for the amazing foreword.

To my brothers and sisters, I would not trade you for anybody or anything; I would choose you over and over if given the opportunity in any life. You are simply the best. Ms. Gloria Osei-Bonsu, you happen to be the first fruit and the peace of the family. Rev. Richies Osei-Bonsu, whose secret name is Duke, you and your beautiful wife, Mrs. Salome Osei-Bonsu, are the pillars of the family. Pastor Ebenezer Osei-Bonsu, a.k.a. Crown Man, you and your beautiful wife, Mrs. Francisca Osei-Bonsu, are the strength of the family. Professor Noble Osei-Bonsu, a.k.a. Le Lee, helped proofread the manuscript. You and your beautiful wife, Mrs. Aku Osei-Bonsu, are the hope of the family. Mrs. Gladys Dzanyikpor, you and your wonderful husband, Mr. Emmanuel Kodjo Dzanyikpor, are the joy of the family. Last but not least, Ms. Joyce Osei-Bonsu, my carbon copy, you are the beauty of the family.

To the strings of my heart, you have stuck with me through thick and thin, and you give me the reason to live: my four boys, Joshua Carlson, Ohene Adom Osei-Bonsu, Otumfuo Ayeyi Osei-Bonsu, and Obrempong Aseda Osei-Bonsu. The future leadership of the world is at your disposal; take it, and make a positive impact.

To the creator of the universe, Yahweh, the sustainer of life and all that pertains to it, be glorified. May You continue to illuminate our minds and path to walk this life with the understanding and the purpose You have for us.

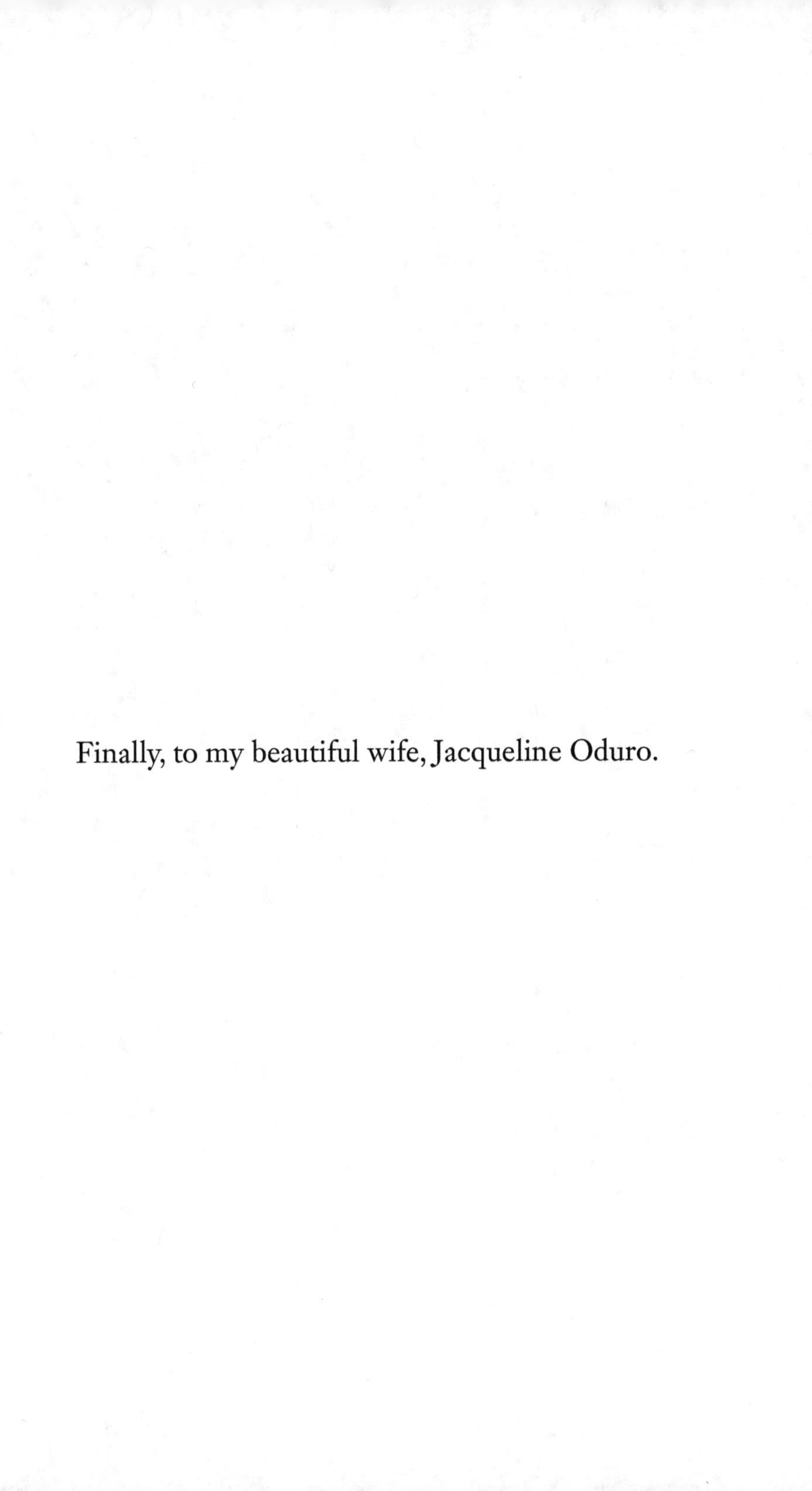

Finally, to my beautiful wife, Jacqueline Oduro.

Introduction

Checking the scholarly definitions of "leadership" in the dictionaries, I was a little taken aback by the fact that all the definitions were playing to the tune of the early Greek philosophers. They thought and taught that leadership is the preserve of a few brilliant people chosen by the gods. In this context, leaders were assumed to be endowed with special qualities that made them uniquely suited to control others. Then it was the ancient monarchs who propagated this definition to legitimize their control over the majority of the people.

The scholarly concept of leadership has destroyed many lives and generations in the world, including Africa. The Greek concept they sold to the world has armed some with the understanding that leadership is charisma and power, and they therefore resort to bullying the least informed or the less privileged in the human society. Others see leadership as a title and a tool to amass a large following, and they thereby resort to manipulation and arm twisting. There are others who also see leadership as control, and they resort to domineering antics in suppressing the very people they claim to be leading. Still others believe that it is ownership and rulership over people, and so they mistreat and control their subordinates. Certain attributes of leadership seem evident in these definitions but may depend on the context of leadership, especially in corporate leadership.

The definition of leadership in our academic literature raises the question, are leaders born or made? At the end of this account, you will realize that no one can make you a leader, but rather we were born leaders to become leaders.

The ancient Greek philosophers believed that you ought to be charismatic to be a leader. "Charisma" means "gifts of the gods"; in other words, leaders are appointed by the gods. These philosophers also believed that to be a leader, you have to be flamboyant and outspoken, so if you didn't possess any of these qualities, you didn't qualify to be a leader; you were born to be led.

This concept of leadership is what has been ingrained into the subconsciousness of Africans, and coupled with our historical experience of colonization and our cultural setting, it makes this gospel the ultimate for them. This leadership concept is entrenched in any monarchical society that has a history of colonization. First of all, monarchies or kingdoms with the intent to rule create a system of ownership of the land and the subjects; therefore, laws are made by the pleasure of the king, so the welfare of the subjects is secondary to the pleasure of the monarch.

Second, colonization creates a system of second-class citizenship made up of rulers and the ruled. Colonization also breaks the spirit of the people; it strips them of their identity, confidence, self-worth, and human dignity and leaves them in a state of brokenness and inferiority. All these ideologies of colonization and kingdoms of rulership are rooted in the ancient Greek concept of leadership, leaving every broken society in search of a savior or a hero.

Leadership is something difficult to explain because it is dynamic. Leadership should be an idea rooted in love or, like beauty, rooted in character. After researching for a while, I couldn't find any definition that conforms to my beliefs, based on God's purpose for man.

The True Purpose of Leadership

Humans are social animals, and as such, we were created to live in a community. Therefore, for the community to live in peace, joy, and harmony and to progress, it needs order, and order produces beauty. All leadership does is to bring order and beauty to our community: "And the Lord God took the man, and put him into the garden of Eden to dress it and to keep it" (Gen. 2:15). This verse sums up all the assignment of humanity and defines leadership. "Dress it and keep it" means to bring order to the world, and that is what our leadership gifts are for.

For man to be fruitful and multiply and to replenish and subdue the earth, he needs the skill of organization, and the leadership seed in us is what gives us the skill for order, management, and organization. In other words, leadership brings order, management, organization, and beauty to our lives and our environment.

Some people have the leadership gift of chemistry, biology, physics, math, and so on to help organize and bring order to the sciences. Some have the leadership gift of writing, teaching, illustrating, and philosophy to organize and bring order to the academics. Some have the leadership gift of poetry, music, fine art, and so forth to organize and bring order to the social aspect of life. Some have the leadership gift of cleaning, recycling, and so on to organize and bring order to our environment.

So, if all of mankind identifies and develops our leadership seeds and serves them to the world, the world will be such an orderly, well-managed, well-organized, and beautiful place. The world is not experiencing the beauty and the orderliness it is supposed to because many people choose not to harness and serve their leadership seeds to the world. This has resulted in a vacuum in the organization, management, and orderliness first in their lives and eventually in the world—hence the ugliness we see all around us.

Discovering your leadership gift puts your life at risk, but understanding the purpose of that gift preserves your life. Just knowing your leadership gift makes you think that the world must serve you because of your gift. No matter what your purpose is, if you understand the world needs you and that the world can't do without your service to humanity, you do whatever you are purposed to do with pride, because no one can do it better than you. It preserves you because, knowing the importance of your role in the world, you would not do anything that would cut your life short.

The following definition of leadership negates the concept of leadership you have learned in the past. Leadership is first personal before it becomes public. I want you to forget about every definition you have read and concentrate on what is going to be expounded on in this book.

Before we begin, I want to debunk the diabolic concept that leadership is the ability to control or rule over people. I just want to establish this fact: no man was born to control or rule over another man. (I am using the word "man" in this book to refer to the spirit of humanity and not as a symbol of gender, so "man" in this context represents both men and women.) This fact of rulership is established in Genesis 1:26, which states, "And God said, let us make man in our own image, after our likeness: and let them have dominion over the fish of the sea, and over the fowl of the air, and over the cattle, and over all the earth, and over every creeping thing that creepeth upon the earth." I believe you would agree with me that of all the things God mentioned, He never said man should have dominion over another man, because the rulership of man is the preserve of God and God alone. This will be discussed in detail later in the book.

Leadership, therefore, is the capacity to influence or have dominion over your environment in your bid to serve humanity with your gift and to lay a good foundation for posterity, which in turn brings you fulfillment. In other words, leadership is the identification and development of one's gift to the service of humanity that brings you fulfillment in life.

Leadership may have different characteristics based on its area of operation, but its fundamental principles remain the same. Any form of leadership must have these three basic components: gift, service to humanity, and fulfillment. Any leadership devoid of any one of these is short of the proper definition of leadership. It may have the form but not its character. This leads us to the next point that leadership is not charisma but character, and leadership without character has no substance. However, leadership can be administered without charisma. A perfect example is Mother Teresa, now Saint Teresa of Calcutta. It is important to note that charisma can only embellish leadership, but it does not make leadership.

Leadership can also be defined as "doing what you were born to do," and this is illustrated in Genesis 2:15: "And the Lord God took the Man, and put him into the garden of Eden to dress it and keep it." This verse gives more insight into the definition of leadership. "Dress it" signifies work, ability, talent, and gift, all which give us the capacity to influence our environment. "Dress it" also means to nurture and cultivate the leadership gift given to man. This indicates that man was created to work. Then again, God commanded man to "keep it," which also indicates that leadership is generational—in other words, whatever you have been gifted to serve your generation must benefit not just you but also generations to come. "Keep it" also means ownership, and ownership means rulership; it also means being a custodian. So, when you dress your gift by cultivating it and nurturing it, then you can keep it in terms of thinking of serving it to generations, so that gives you the capacity to control or rule over the environment in the service of humanity. In conclusion, leadership is first self-discovery, because you cannot serve without first knowing what you are serving or having nothing to serve. The day you discover what you were born to do marks the beginning of your leadership journey. Concisely, leadership is your gift for service to humanity. You don't attain leadership; you unwrap it. In other words, it is not something you work to achieve; you already have it. Just find it and develop it. Leadership is neither an office nor a title, but it's the *gift* of occupying an office. Titles could be dangerous, as titles are earned, but leadership is a gift. Titles can never earn you leadership, but leadership will always earn you a title.

We often misconstrue the power of leadership to mean the ability of leadership to do anything it pleases. There are two dimensions of power or authority as far as leadership is concerned. There is the power or the authority of the leadership office and the power or the authority of the leadership gift. The power of the leadership office is derived from the power of the gift. Before I go further, I want to define power or authority, and in my own words, power is the ability to perform, and in the context of leadership, it is the ability to perform service. This means, in the performance of service, authority is derived in the area of your gift or talent. So, for instance, the auto mechanic is an authority when it comes to fixing automobiles, because of his or her gift with which the community is served. The gift in the person carries an authority, and then by providing service to the community an office is created for the gift, and now the office of the mechanic also carries an authority.

So now, when the community has an automobile problem, they will go to the office of the auto mechanic, which is an authority they trust, but then they also trust in the authority of John Doe or Jane Doe who has the gift to run the office. Therefore, the authority or the power of leadership is based on trust, and the legitimate authority is vested in one's ability to serve. For instance, the police officer's authority is in his or her service and the community's trust in the authority of the police officer to protect the community. So, if the legitimate authority of leadership is not in service, it becomes just another force, which can be converted into coercion or compulsion. Therefore, we always have to make sure that the authority of the leadership gift is running the authority of the leadership office. This is where the misunderstanding of the authority or power of leadership is misused. The authority of leadership is rooted in service and trust, so when the leadership authority loses its trust and service, it becomes reckless and abusive.

The relationship between the authority or power of leadership, the service of leadership and the gift of leadership, is synonymous with the Trinity. God the Father is synonymous with the authority of leadership, God the Son is to the service of leadership, and God the Holy Spirit is the gift of leadership. They operate interdependently, they cannot be separated in their functions. They are interrelated, they cannot be separated in their functions.

Influence in the context of leadership has two dimensions. First is the influence you have on your environment, systems, and circumstances, which you use to the advantage of the service to society. In other words, by virtue of your role, you are able to influence the environment to the advantage of humanity. For example, when a leader in the business field creates a job for the poor to make ends meet, he has exercised his influence of leadership over the system of poverty to the benefit of humanity. This is where our control or dominion over the environment and not over people comes in.

Second, when people get attracted to your gift, they respect your opinion on issues concerning your area of gifting. So you have an influence on their perception as far as your area of gifting is concerned, and this is where you have the responsibility to influence their perception rightfully. The people get attracted to you because of your gift, so the emphasis here is the gift and not you. A clear analogy here is that we go to the tree to get the fruit and not to admire the tree.

You can influence humanity only through your service, so leadership is not the influence but the service. Your influence is derived from your service to humanity.

Before we delve into this question, let us go back to Genesis 1:26: "God said, 'Let us make man in our own image, after our likeness.'" There are two very important words here: "image" and "likeness." Let's first look at the word "image." It means the exact reflection of one's self, like when you look in the mirror, you see the exact reflection of yourself, so we wouldn't be wrong to say that God looks like man. Then the word "likeness" refers to like characteristics, behaviors, attributes, abilities, natures, or actions. So in both reflection and in actions, man is like God.

Let us take a look at the likeness or the nature of God, one of which is leadership. God created man, so God will rule over man, and man will rule over the systems of the world. His creative power is also one of His likeness or ability; therefore, man, in the likeness of God, is also a leader and a creator. God made man His cocreator, as demonstrated in Genesis 2:19–20: "And out of the ground the Lord God formed every beast of the field, and every fowl of the air, and brought them unto Adam to see what he would call them: and whatsoever

Adam called every living creature, that was the name thereof. And Adam gave names to all cattle, and to the fowl of the air, and to every beast of the field; but for Adam there was not found an help meet for him."

There are two major points to take note of in this verse. First, God addressed man by name; all along He was referring to him as man. This time He was dealing with the human man and not the spirit man. He translated creation from the spirit to the physical, indicating that Adam, who is human just like any name, has the ability to function like God.

Second, the verse says that whatever Adam called the creatures, that was the name thereof, and not "that became the name." In other words, Adam was in the likeness of God, so he knew the names God intended for every animal, and he just called them what God had in mind.

"And the Lord God formed man of the dust of the ground, and breathed into his nostrils the breath of life; and man became a living soul" (Gen. 2:7). This indicates that man possesses not just the reflection of God but also the life breath of God that produces the characteristics of God. Breath signifies life, and the life of a being is the very nature of that being. One of the major attributes of leadership is creative ability—leaders will always create something out of nothing; leaders always venture into the unknown—and that is synonymous with God.

Since every man is created in the likeness of God, it suggests that every man born on earth has within him the spirit of leadership. We were all born to be leaders, to subdue our environment with our gifts, and to serve humanity. No one was born to be a follower. We become followers when we settle for jobs instead of doing the work we were born to do. A job makes you a follower, but work makes you a leader. *Work* is that which you were born to do, and a *job* is that which you do to survive. Work is defined as what you have been gifted to do to serve humanity for life's fulfillment.

Based on the definition of work, let's take a look at the similarities between work and leadership. Based on the leadership definition discussed earlier, we realize that three features are highlighted in both definitions: gift, service to humanity, and fulfillment. These elements can also be seen in creation by God: His gift is His ability to create. His service to humanity was that He created all things for humanity. And fulfillment is reflected in His declaration that all He had created was good. In Genesis 1:31 we read, "And God saw everything that he had made, and, behold, it was very good. And the evening and the morning were the sixth day. God, being the greatest leader, exhibited these three major features in his work, and since man was created in his image and likeness, man must also exhibit these three major features in his work to reflect God's image. In conclusion, we can say that leadership is the work you were born to do, and since every man was assigned a work to do, every man was born a leader."

Understanding the Principle of Work: The Difference between Work and Job

Because God wanted man to understand the concept and the principle of work, He withheld rain until He created man: "And every plant of the field before it was in the earth, and every herb of the field before it grew: for the Lord God had not caused it to rain upon the earth, and *there was* not a man to till the ground" (Gen. 2:5). So the only thing that validates the existence of man is work, and anything that allows you to get wealth without work, such as the lottery, is a violation of God's purpose. In other words, any ideology that guarantees you wealth without work is folly.

This also means that praying for wealth without working is a violation of the principle of work and undermines human dignity, as it is stated in 2 Thessalonians 3:10: "For even when we were with you, this we commanded you, that if any would not work, neither should he eat." When you really pray, as I know prayer to be a communion between man and God, then you should be wise because, then, He will communicate to you His wisdom and the deep things of God. If you always pray and you are still foolish, believing in some of these untruths about work, then you should check the existence of the God you are in communication with or examine your prayer to see if it is a monologue or a dialogue. You cannot have a healthy dialogue with the Most High God and remain foolish.

In a job, you may not have a gift, but you may have an ability, which may be derived from learning a trade, though you may still lack the skill that comes with the gift. Also, the primary motive or intent of a job is selfish. You may not like the job, but you will do it because it is going to help you fulfill your ambition of paying your bills or living the lifestyle you crave—not because it will serve humanity. Finally, it does not give you true fulfillment since you always dread going to the job and always wish it were Friday.

Jobs are the reason you are surviving, and work is the reason you were born. That is why you can always be relieved of your job, but you can never be relieved of your work. Your work is that which you are gifted to do, but your job is what you learn to do. You don't teach a bird to fly because that is what it was created to do. In that same vein, your work defines you, and you cannot be separated from your work because that is who you are.

Jobs were first introduced to man when God was pronouncing a curse in Genesis: "Cursed is the ground for thy sake; in sorrow shalt thou eat of it all the days of thy life. Thorns also and thistles shall it bring forth to thee; and thou shall eat the herb of the field. In the sweat of thy face shalt thou eat bread" (Gen. 3:17–19). First of all, realize that God continually spoke about sweating to eat bread. We will struggle to survive, and that is the reason we take a job—just to survive. This is different from the work God gave to man in Genesis 2:15 when He said, "Dress it and keep it." Here God's emphasis was on cultivating and nurturing, which require gift and skill. In the case of sweating to eat, it implies that you may do anything you can just to eat, and this may not require any gift or skill. So jobs were a curse to man for not doing the work God gave him; instead, man was busy trying to be like God, forgetting that he was already made like God. When the devil said, "Man can be like God when he eats the fruit," he meant that man can be like God in the area of rulership over another man, which the devil knew very well was the preserve of God and God alone. Moreover, God has made man like Himself to rule over the earth and his environment, in the area of purpose and creativity, for God to get the glory.

If you don't realize what you have, you will be wandering about looking for what you already have, and that will lead you to violate your purpose.

The success of any entity is defined by its purpose, so your success in life is defined by the fulfillment of your purpose. Knowing your purpose without understanding your assignment can lead you to destruction. No matter who you are, whether you were born legitimately or illegitimately, planned or unplanned, in or out of wedlock, rich or poor, you were born for a specific assignment, and that assignment is your leadership gift.

Discovering and fulfilling your assignment in life does not necessarily mean you will be financially wealthy, but one thing is assured, and that is you are going to be fulfilled. You were born to fulfill a specific assignment no one else could do; you are the only person equipped for that assignment, and that is how unique you are. Come to think of it, there are more than seven billion people in this world and more than seven billion different sets of fingerprints; there are no two fingerprints alike. So, if you refuse to carry out your assignment, guess what? It will not get done, and I always say that the world will never be the same with or without you. If you decide not to do anything, the world will not be the same, and if you decide to influence your generation, the world will not be the same—think about it.

Your uniqueness is encapsulated in your purpose, which is why you don't have to be like anybody else. You may look like somebody, but you can never be him or her, the same way nobody can be you, even though he or she may look like you. You may try to be like somebody else, but remember you will not have the gift to support that image. You have the gift and potentials only to support your image. As a matter of fact, the world needs you, and if you lose your identity, the world will lose you, because there is only one of you in the world. No matter how hard you try, you cannot outperform the original, and that will always make you the second best. Why do you want to be the second best when you can be second to none? When you put a bird in water, it will struggle to survive because it has been placed in an environment where it does not have the gift or the potential to excel. Your uniqueness is buried in your DNA; it goes beyond your physical appearance or your social status.

When you go for a job interview, be yourself, and don't try to be what the employers are looking for. If you are not what they are looking for, move on. If you force yourself into that environment, you may not have the gift to excel, and you may end up getting fired—or worse, being unfulfilled.

There is a true story about a woman named Lillian Tinsley who decided to fulfill her assignment, and let's see the generational effect. The Blake family, who lived in New York in the early 1940s, was struggling to make ends meet, so Henry Blake decided to drop out of school at the age of sixteen to work and support his struggling mother financially. There was a church member by the name of Lillian Tinsley, an elderly woman who had no family of her own but loved the young people in the church. Ms. Tinsley was a domestic helper in the neighborhood and was making a very limited income. She heard about Henry and told his mother to send him back to school, and she would give the Blake family out of her limited income what Henry could have made from working. Ms. Tinsley helped to see Henry Blake through college in Alabama.

Because of Lillian Tinsley's decision to fulfill her leadership assignment, Dr. Herman Blake and his family are now contributing immensely to the development of humanity. Ms. Lillian Tinsley was not occupying any position of power and probably had no charisma, but she was a leader who ruled over a system of poverty affecting a family to do what, I believe, she was born to do. I have no doubt in my mind that this was her life's purpose because had she not risen to this leadership occasion, what do you think would have happened to the Blake family and the impact Dr. Blake is now making on humanity? Dr. Blake has contributed greatly to the academic world, especially in the area of sociology.

Do not underestimate your leadership seed, for no assignment is too small. If you want to be fulfilled in life, do what gives you joy, even if you are not paid. A whole generation may be jeopardized because you chose not to fulfill your assignment in life.

Sometimes your assignment may be discovered in the midst of adversity. You might be right in the midst of your purpose and may not know you have been equipped to fulfill that particular assignment. Let's take a look at a young man who was equipped to liberate the nation of Israel and did not even know it. He was standing right at the threshold of his leadership assignment and had no clue but instead was complaining.

In Judges 6–8, Gideon had a visitor who referred to him as a mighty man of valor (Judg. 6:12). "And Gideon said unto him, oh my Lord, if the Lord be with us, why then is all this befallen us? And where be all his miracles our fathers told us of, saying, did not the Lord bring us up from Egypt? But now the Lord hath forsaken us, and delivered us into the hands of the Midianites" (Judg. 6:13). Gideon was the very miracle he was questioning God about, and he didn't even know it. Even though Gideon was nobody in the land of Israel—as a matter of fact, he was from a very poor village and a very poor family in the land of Israel—he was being referred to as a mighty man of valor.

This proves that your purpose in life is not defined by your current state but by what has been deposited in you. Adversities are opportunities for you to manifest your abilities; they are not meant to destroy you but are meant to introduce you to your purpose in life. In the midst of war and famine in Israel, Gideon, a mighty warrior and the miracle Israel was looking for, was revealed.

How to Become the Leader
You Were Born to Be

To begin this chapter, I want to emphasize this: no man on earth can make you who you were born to be. You were born a leader, your leadership seed is already deposited in you, and you may be a follower now because you have not yet discovered you. All anybody or any learning does is to help grow you into who you already are. Remember, the sunlight, the water, and the soil do not make the orange tree, but they help process and grow the tree.

Very often you hear people saying they don't know what their purpose in life is, or they don't know what they were born to do in life, or they don't know how to go about discovering their purpose in life. In the history of humanity, there are four major questions being asked by every man irrespective of race, creed, sex, social status, or position in life. They are the following:

1. Who is man? This question has to do with the identity of man.

2. Where from man? This question focuses on the origin of man.
3. Why man? This question deals with the purpose of man.
4. Where does man go from here? This question deals with the destiny of man.

Always avoid the path of least resistance to answer these questions. The more resistant your path is, the more you sharpen your leadership qualities.

The first question of identity is one of the major struggles of humanity. "Who am I" was the major reason man sinned against God in the garden. If man knew who he was, he would have defeated the serpent. When the serpent told Adam and Eve that they would be like God the day they ate the fruit of the tree, their response should have been, "We are already like God, because He made us in His image and likeness." The truth is that you don't have to be like anybody to be a leader. As a matter of fact, you can never be a leader if you want to be like somebody else because that will make you a counterfeit and not original. Counterfeits are followers and not leaders. Originals lead.

The false identification of you by society leads to an identity crisis. Most of the time, we confuse the content with the package, and society labels the package and makes us think that decorating the package gives us value. So we go about putting tags on the package, wanting to be like others, forgetting that the value is on the content and not the package.

In our quest to decorate the package, we tend to be caricatures as a result of an identity crisis. We can trace most of the problems we have in our world today—killings, backbiting, cheating, jealousy, drug addiction, hate, forgiveness, you name it—to an identity crisis. People will do anything just to be recognized by society. People who are too egoistic are suffering from an identity crisis. If you know who you are, you don't seek the approval of society, and yet society will recognize you because the content of the package gives it value, so if you want to be valued by society, show them the content.

Your identity has nothing to do with your facial beauty or your height or your build or your complexion—it has nothing to do with your outward being. When you find your identity, you will discover your worth, and your worth leads you to your purpose so that you can press on to your fulfilled destination. Your identity gives you value, and it leads you to a place of eternal memorial, where you live in the minds and the hearts of humanity forever, because it will cause you to leave your footprints in the sands of time.

Your identity is the image of your work you were born to do, and when you reveal your identity to the world, it becomes a tag of value you carry on you. No matter how small you may think your identity is, it has enormous value to put you in a place of eternal memorial. In Matthew 26:6–13, a woman poured a bottle of expensive ointment on the feet of Jesus and wiped them with her hair. The disciples complained about it, and Jesus said to them, "Verily I say unto you, wheresoever this gospel shall be preached in the whole world, there shall also this, that this woman hath done, be told for a memorial of her" (Matt. 26:13). The moment you mention the names of some musicians, such as Michael Jackson, Bob Marley, or Whitney Houston, their identity with music is what first comes to mind. They found their identity and served it to the world, so even though they have been dead for years now, their identity still lives on.

The moment you find your identity—no matter what your name is, no matter who gave birth to you, no matter what your background is, no matter what color your skin is, no matter how beautiful or ugly you are—the world will love you and will recognize your existence.

Often society defines us, and we settle for that. Society tells us that we have to be like someone else to be accepted, which is a lie from the pit of hell. Until you discover who you are, you will always be a people pleaser and do what others want you to do and will never be able to do that which you want to do. You always become a slave to those who define your life. Comparing what happened in the garden to the temptation of Jesus Christ by the same old serpent, Jesus knew who he was, so he refused the devil with the word of God. To know who you are, you must first understand that you are a product of God, and every product manufactured comes with a written manual. In the case of man, your manual is the Bible. Genesis tells you who you are as a product of God in His own image and likeness and that you possess within your being the creative power and the abilities of God for a specific assignment on earth. This concept alone makes you feel different; it exudes some confidence and pride in you and makes you start thinking differently. The moment you get this concept of your identity, you start probing into your source and your assignment, which leads you to the next question of origin.

The second question mankind has been struggling with is the origin of man. In Genesis it was recorded that man is the very breath and life of God; in other words, man has to function like God. When man aligns himself with God, man can know what is in God's mind as it happened in the Garden of Eden. When God brought the animals to Adam to see what he would name them, Adam did not give them his names; he gave them names God had intended for them. Because Adam was in tune with his source, the creator, he knew the mind of God. And for you to know that your source is God will encourage you to want to know why God created you with such beauty and awesomeness.

The question of meaning, or the purpose for man, or the purpose of man, is another big question that has been bothering mankind for ages. Man was created to manage and rule the earth, and to some people, the bigger question is in finding their area of rulership. If you go back to the beginning, the scripture says in Genesis 1:26, "God said, let us make man in our own image and let them have dominion over the earth." God wants to rule the earth through man, so for that purpose, He created a being like Himself who can exhibit God's glory on earth. What we are going to attempt to do in this book is to assist those struggling to identify their area of rulership.

The fourth and final question of man is where man is going from here, and this is twofold: one is life after death, which is not going to be tackled in this book, and the other is the destiny of purpose, which will be discussed in this book. The destiny of purpose deals with what you were born to do or to become as well as the process to achieve and fulfill that purpose. First of all, you have to understand that God is a master architect; He always plans His things to the end before starting them—just like an architect of a building who puts the building first on paper and knows what the building is going to look like, the number of rooms it is going to have, where the kitchen is going to be located, where the bedrooms are going to be, and so forth. So, before a building is erected, the architect has already seen it, and that is how God works. Digging the foundation is the beginning of a building that has already been completed. Before you were born, God had already planned your life, so you were born to begin that which He had already ended. Therefore, your birth is a sign of your success.

In Genesis 1 God had already spelled out what He intended for man to do, even before He created man. Another typical example can be found in Jeremiah 1:5: "Before I formed thee in the belly I knew thee; and before thou camest forth out of the womb I sanctified thee, and I ordained thee a prophet unto the nations." This clearly tells us that before you were born, God had already assigned a purpose to your life, and He has in His plan what exactly He wants you to do. He then deposits the seed of your purpose in you, in the form of gifting for us to fulfill that assignment. Every life on earth has an assignment to fulfill, and everything on earth has a purpose. And the fact that we don't know it does not mean it has no purpose, because God will not allow any life or a thing on earth without any purpose or any assignment. Any entity on earth has an assigned purpose to it—even unborn babies, either planned or unplanned.

Discovering your purpose or assignment in life that also puts you on your way to your destination is very critical in life. Becoming the leader you were born to be, or discovering the work you were born to do, can be influenced by two backdrops: your environment and your circumstances.

Your environment consists of your birth and upbringing—your geographical location, your parents, your siblings, your school, and your friends will help shape your belief system and your perceptions in life. This plays a large role in identifying your leadership seed in life. If you are placed in the right environment, it is easy to identify your assignment, sometimes at a very tender age of your life. An example of this is Michael Jackson, who was born into a musical family, and because the father had an interest in the music, he decided to help the members of the Jackson Five to develop their musical gifts. Out of this Michael Jackson was produced and became one of the biggest music icons the world has ever known.

Let's look at this from another angle, though. What if the father was not interested in the music and decided to shut it down? Or what if Michael Jackson was born into a family of carpenters or shoemakers? He probably would have ended up a frustrated and unfulfilled carpenter or shoemaker and would have left a huge vacuum in the music world.

Sometimes the extracurricular activities in school, be it playing sports or learning a musical instrument, can help shape your choices based on the seed deposited in you. That is why parenting is very important in helping in the early identification and development of your leadership seed. Parents are one of the early instruments you need in shaping your life in the direction of your assignment.

The other backdrop influencing the identification of purpose or assignment in life is circumstances. The circumstances are the situations one finds himself or herself in either by choice or fate, foreseen or unforeseen. Some of the circumstances are poverty, oppression, disappointments, and any setbacks you could think of. In this scenario, it is very easy to give up and walk away from your purpose or your destiny. Any of these situations, however, can become a springboard for those who are mentally prepared, those who have fed their minds with positive thoughts. People who emerge from their circumstances are mostly character proven because they usually take the time to shape their character by the circumstances they find themselves in.

Nelson Mandela is an example of a man who discovered his purpose in life through circumstances. Nelson Mandela grew up in an oppressed system, so his leadership character was shaped by his experience, and that is why he was such a unique president. Even though he studied to become a lawyer, his circumstances shaped him to be a liberator. His character was shaped to understand that oppression is evil and that it was not fun being on the receiving end, so he decided not to put anybody in that situation. Dr. David Abdulai of Shekinah Clinic in Ghana was another example of a man who found his purpose in a setback circumstance. He grew up in a very poor environment and determined to find his purpose in life and fulfill it in the service of humanity. He saw what the system of poverty could do to humanity firsthand, which made him mad, and he vowed to rule over the system of poverty.

To prevail in circumstances of adversity, you first have to come to terms with the first two questions of life: your identity and your origin. As a matter of fact, answering these two questions for those in this situation is vital in their pursuit of purpose or assignment for their lives, whereas people in the environment scenario don't really bother to answer those two questions since it is not a motivational factor for them.

Bear in mind, neither of these backdrops is better than the other; they both have a way of shaping you into fulfilling your purpose. Everything exists for a reason, and I mean everything that you call a problem has a purpose in your life, and your job is to find that purpose and fulfill it. Leaders don't just solve problems, but they fulfill the purpose of the problems they face. Sometimes walking away from a problem solves it, but it does not fulfill the purpose of the problem. Every problem you face is meant for your success. For those who know the truth, a setback is just a setup for success.

We are going to address two groups in this section: those who are still struggling to identify their leadership gifts or their purposes in life and those who have identified their leadership gifts or purposes in life but are struggling to fulfill or bring them to fruition due to the circumstances they find themselves in or confronting them.

To discover your purpose in life or your leadership seed, you must first deal with your thinking process. Your mind is like the womb, and your thoughts are like the sperm, so any thought you put into your mind will be incubated and processed into belief, then it becomes a concept or idea; then in its final trimester, it becomes an attitude, which is birth into action. Attitude will drive you toward your purpose in life. Your attitude is very vital in this journey of life. Feeding your mind with the right information is the key because whatever you feed your mind with will be processed into your attitude. Feed your mind with the truth, and your attitude will produce the true attitude of you. If you feed your mind with the wrong and incorrect information, it will produce a false attitude of you.

The lion is classified as the king of the jungle even though he is neither the biggest nor the tallest animal in the jungle. The lion is neither the strongest nor the fastest, but one thing sets him apart, and that is his attitude. A lion creates a territory, and he rules in that territory, and no other animal is permitted in that domain. Any time the lion sees another animal, he does not consider it a threat, but all he sees is food, and with that attitude, he overpowers his prey for food.

Another unique animal with the attitude of a leader is the eagle. The eagle has a fearless attitude of a conqueror, and that is what earned it the title "king of birds." Whenever there is lightning and thunder, all other birds flee; the eagle is the only bird that soars toward the lightning and flies above it to reach a higher altitude.

Attitude is vital if you want to do that which you were born to do. With this understanding, you must first acknowledge that your identity is in God as you were created in His image and likeness. Then you also have to understand that you originate from God for a specific assignment. You must begin to think that you were born to make a difference, as it is recorded in Proverbs 23:7: "For as he thinketh in his heart, so is he."

Now, begin by asking yourself, "What was I born to do, and what can I do to make the world a better place?" Then give yourself an assignment by telling yourself that you will not leave this world until you fulfill every purpose of God concerning your life. The other right thing to do is to go to the manufacturer to ask Him to help you find your purpose. If you have an iPhone and you don't know its use, the right thing to do is to go to the manufacturer, Apple, for answers. In most cases the manufacturer has a manual you can refer to. So go to God, who is the manufacturer in this case, and ask for help. Then you refer to His manual for life, which is the Bible, for guidance.

The next thing you do is to find a quiet place where there will be no interruptions and begin to think about your life in retrospect as far back as you can remember. This step requires a lot of deep thinking, analysis, and brainstorming. It is advisable to be by yourself and stay away from anything that will distract you. Begin to think of the childhood dreams you had, because in most cases, those childhood dreams are authentic and pure because they are not motivated by money.

Sometimes dreams are killed at that age by people around you; your leadership seed might seem too big for them to conceptualize. And when you were talked out of certain dreams, it was a reminder of all the reasons you couldn't fulfill those dreams. Not all those naysayers meant evil; some may have feared seeing you hurt or getting disappointed. But hold on to your dreams and remember what you were born to do. Your purpose in life does not necessarily mean you are going to be rich and famous, but no matter what, aim to be fulfilled at the end of each day.

I remember asking an eleven-year-old boy in a village in Ghana, West Africa, what he wanted to do when he grew up, and his response was to be a doctor. My follow-up question was *why* he wanted to be a doctor, and his response was so pure and genuine when he said, "I want to help dying people." This is so sacred. Most times at that age, whenever you see someone doing what you were born to do, it awakens some emotional connection in you, "deep calleth unto deep." In Psalm 42:7, as it is recorded, "Deep calleth unto deep at the noise of thy waterspouts: all thy waves and thy billows are gone over me." This means that even if you are in your worst state in life, that which is deposited in you will always recognize and want to respond to a similar sound on the outside. Most of the time, when you realize what you were born to be, it scares you, but at that age, you are so authentic that nothing scares you, and all you know is this is what you want to do.

That is why Jesus said in Matthew 19:14, "Suffer little children, and forbid them not, to come unto me: for of such is the kingdom of heaven." All He is saying is that if you want to enjoy the peace and the joy of life, if you want to live the life you have been destined to live, then you have to be bold and fearless to do that which you are dreaming of. If you are struggling to identify what you were born to do, do not ignore your childhood years. The thoughts you had then are vital in leading you to your destiny. One thing you have to remember, though, is that society will always define you by your current conditions, but God will always define you by the potentials He deposited in you.

After you identify a couple of things you wanted to do when you were a child, the next step is to measure them against your potentials. What this means is to think of what you can do currently (1) with joy because you love doing it and it makes you happy doing it, (2) without any struggles because it comes to you naturally and you have the flare for it, and (3) with love even if you are not being paid. Pay attention to every detail, and don't take any of those details for granted. It could be that you love to smile and always make sure that people are comfortable around you, which is in line with customer service, nursing, community service, and many more occupations. You may love to advise others, help them solve their problems, and help them fulfill the purpose of their problems, and this might be in line with the work of a counselor. You may also have been inquisitive as a child, following after every event in town and bringing the news to your family and friends, and this might be in line with journalism or media work. If you were very funny growing up as a child—wherever you went, you made people laugh—this might be in line with comedy. No matter what you come up with, remember the three most important elements here: doing it with joy, doing it without any struggles, and potentially doing it free of charge.

The next step is to seek counsel from a sound and progressive member of your community to assist you in figuring out how to identify your gift. The best people will be your parents or any older person who was around you when growing up, or it could be a mentor, your pastor, or a community leader. "Where no counsel is, the people fall: but in the multitude of counsellors there is safety" (Prov. 11:14). At this stage you must be resolute and determine that no one can talk you out of this journey, so you have to be careful whom you confide in. You can be rest assured that if you do these steps thoroughly, you will find what you were born to do, your leadership seed.

The next step is to fine-tune that gift by taking the necessary steps to develop that leadership seed. You need information, which is vital in the development of your gift. That could include receiving formal or informal education, reading, and becoming a critical thinker. Critical thinking means probing for solutions by analyzing and questioning possible solutions to arrive at a very thoughtful and meticulous solution. You also need to identify a mentor in the field you are pursuing, someone who will teach you the ropes and the ins and outs of the field. You also need to surround yourself with other critical thinkers who are more experienced than you. Make sure you are not the most experienced and knowledgeable person in your circle of friends. In that case, if you are confronted with a challenge, you can look up to a friend. This also means you have to select your friends carefully because the friends you keep can help you develop or abort your leadership seed. For example, if you hang out with friends who abuse drugs, there is the possibility that you could be introduced to drugs that could ruin your life.

Always endeavor to make wise decisions, which can be made only from thinking analytically and not from emotions. Don't be in a hurry to make a decision or a choice; always take your time and ponder over your choices. Analyze your options before choosing one. Some decisions when made are gone and cannot be recalled, and sometimes it will take you years if not forever to repair the damage caused by those decisions.

This brings us to the issue of mistakes in life. Rule number one: never allow your mistakes to hold you down, because mistakes are part of life's test book. We should study our mistakes to solve life's problems and by fulfilling the purpose of the problems. Rule number two: don't be scared to make mistakes, because they make you wiser. The only failure in life is not trying to do anything for fear of making a mistake.

4

Attaining the Act of Leadership

There seems to be an eternal debate about whether leaders are born or made. In as much as we were all born with a leadership seed, we must learn to become the leaders we were born to be. Otherwise, we will die followers with leadership seeds trapped in us. You see, God sets our destiny, and it is our responsibility to pursue it. To become a good leader, you must always learn about and be abreast of current issues in your field. Learning is part of leadership, and you must learn to perfect the attributes of leadership to reflect the true image of leadership. For instance, you must learn to be humble and patient at all times. You must learn to be merciful, you must learn to be honest, and you must learn to discipline yourself. You must also learn to listen and to perceive *good* from *right* at all times—that is, what is good may not necessarily be right. For example, eating junk food may be good to kill your hunger, but it may not be the right food for your health. What is right may not also necessarily be good—for instance, refusing to take a bribe that might be needed to solve a pressing family need is the right thing to do, but it may not feel good.

Second Timothy 2:15 says, "Study to shew thyself approved unto God, a workman that needeth not be ashamed, rightly dividing the word of truth."

As we have already established, leadership is the work you were born to do. Apostle Paul stated clearly in 2 Timothy 2:15 that you need to study to show yourself approved unto God for the work He has entrusted in your care for the service of humanity. In other words, for you to be successful in your leadership pursuit, learn to perfect your leadership attributes of humility, patience, self-discipline, and righteousness. By the way, righteousness simply means always standing for what is right. By so doing, you will not be ashamed for falling short of what is expected of you as far as patience is concerned. By so doing, you will not be ashamed for falling short of what is expected of you as far as having mercy on the less fortunate is concerned. By so doing, you will not be ashamed for falling short of what is expected of you as far as humility is concerned. By so doing, you will not be ashamed for falling short of what is expected of you as far as doing what is right against doing good is concerned. You know, doing a good thing may not always be right, and a good leader should always be able to discern when to do the right thing.

In Philippians 4:11–12, again the apostle Paul said, "Not that I speak in respect of want: for I have learned, in whatsoever state I am, therewith to be content. I know both how to be abased, and I know how to abound: everywhere and in all things, I am instructed both to be full and to be hungry, both to abound and to suffer need." This is a very powerful and bold statement; you can make this statement only if you really understand your leadership responsibilities. One very important word in this passage is "learned." As spiritual as Paul was, I was expecting him to say, "By the grace of God, or by the Holy Spirit, in whatsoever state I am content," but instead he said, "I have *learned* to be content." So being content, which is an attribute of character, must be learned. In other words, you can never pray into being what you must learn. Spirituality has its place and so does learning; all the apostle is saying is that we have to learn the act of self-discipline. We have to subject our will to principles that will build in us character that will uphold justice in the face of temptation. I define character as the fortitude to resist injustice, to uphold truth, and to do the right thing even when it is not convenient. Character is the very soul of leadership; therefore, leadership without character is like a moving vehicle with no driver—it is reckless and dangerous.

No matter which leadership field you are in, you are going to be defined by your leadership character. If you are a leader in the auto mechanic field and you understand your leadership role to humanity as Apostle Paul did, you will never repair a broken part to fix a vehicle for which you have been paid to replace. To build character, you need to cultivate the principles of leadership.

Since leadership is a service, there are three major attributes of leadership you must learn to be successful. Without these three foundational pillars, you will be found wanting, and it will be difficult if not impossible for you to serve. These are humility, selflessness, and the tenacity to fight. When I say fight, I don't mean fighting people—you will be constantly fighting circumstances, systems, obstacles, and your own negative tendencies.

In the gospel of John 13:1–17, Jesus defined leadership in its simplest terms: "Verily, verily, I say unto you, the servant is not greater than his lord; neither he that is sent greater than he that sent him" (John 13:16). This is the summary of leadership; all the master is saying here is that the servant and the Lord are the same, and none is greater than the other. He simply is making a distinction between the act and the office. The servant is the act of leadership, and the Lord is the office of leadership. So if you are an auto mechanic, for instance, your office that is the Lord is the auto mechanic that enables you to serve your community. Also, your office might be as important as the Lord, so you ought to have the attributes of a servant to serve humanity as a leader. So the Lord, which is the office, is empty without the servant, which is the act or the definition. The lesson here is that you can never be a leader without service, because leadership is service, and you cannot serve if you are not humble.

Humility doesn't just happen; you have to learn to submit your ego to the authority of love. "He riseth from supper, and laid aside his garments; and took a towel, and girded himself. After that he poureth water into a bason, and began to wash the disciples' feet, and to wipe them with the towel wherewith he was girded" (John 13:4–5). In this chapter the

Master washed the feet of His disciples, which is a sign of humility, and then He demonstrated the difference between the office of leadership and the acts of leadership. He took off his garment, which signifies His office (the Lord), and stepped into the shoes of a servant to fulfill the purpose of the office, which is the act. In this case, any privileges allocated to the office are for the office and not because of the individual. It is also not because the individual occupying the office is more important than any other person. It simply means that the person occupying the office has an increase in his or her responsibilities, so some of the assignment has to be delegated. You have to submit your ego to the power of love with the understanding that it is just a privilege given to you to serve.

The act of selflessness is one other important attribute of leadership. South African President Nelson Mandela said it best: "There can be no greater gift than that of giving one's time and energy to help others without expecting anything in return." In the same vein, Rev. Dr. Martin Luther King said, "If you've got nothing worth dying for, you've got nothing worth living for." These statements tell you that selflessness is an integral part of leadership, which is the highest form of sacrifice. Therefore, you have to cultivate the act of selflessness, and one way of doing that is to learn to help people without any reward. You can start from your home, taking on chores without being asked to and doing them with joy. In other words, your purpose is worth your life.

There is a saying that charity begins at home, and it is very true that the home has a tremendous impact in shaping our perspectives in life. The home is where your leadership training begins. Helping your immediate family selflessly and learning to pick up chores willingly without complaint is a way of developing that selfless nature. It is easy to be of service to your immediate family, and after a while, it becomes a habit, or a lifestyle, of serving others.

Always let your children understand that any time you ask them to do a chore, they should not look at who else is or is not doing what. Teach them service to humanity, because their home is their world. If leadership is service, then service is always to humanity and not about the server. Any time a leader in the restaurant field wakes up in the morning, he thinks of how he could find good and healthy products to cook a good and healthy meal to serve the community. This he sees as his contribution to assist in creating a healthy community, and the monetary profit takes a back seat in his mind. What gives him fulfillment is when the community attributes the reduction of their health problems to his healthy meals.

The third most important pillar of leadership is the ability to fight. First of all, you need to develop the fortitude to fight any resistance to the development of your leadership seed, even before you start leading. To be successful as a leader, you have to be fighting the whole time. You will be fighting injustice, wrong perceptions, institutions, systems, wrong traditions, and even your own negative tendencies. This is to say that you need to develop the character to resist injustices and wrongs in your community and to push to defend justice and truth to establish the right to humanity. If you are a leader in the business field, you will constantly be fighting the system of underpaying people for their work done or the system of tax evasion or the system of relabeling expired goods to prolong its illegal life-span. There is also the possibility of fighting overinvoicing and underinvoicing. Whatever area of leadership you find yourself in, there are some fights you may be forced to put up with to uphold the truth and the dignity of humanity.

Again, as the saying goes, this fighting spirit can be cultivated from the home. Learn to defend the truth and the vulnerable members of your family. One of the things you can do to motivate yourself to take a position to defend the truth whenever you are confronted with the choice is to ask yourself this question: "If I don't make the right choice, what will happen to humanity?" As was asserted by Dr. King in his message "I've Been to the Mountaintop" on April 3, 1968, in Memphis, Tennessee, he believed the Good Samaritan who saw a wounded man asked the same question—"If I don't stop to help this man, what will happen to him?" The priest and the Levites, he believed, asked the question in reverse: "If I stop to help this man, what will happen to me?" Most times people refuse to fight because they ask the wrong question, but leaders will always ask, "If I don't stop to do the right thing, what will happen to humanity?"

Any leader with a fighting spirit does not know failure or calamity. As a matter of fact, the only failure in life is not attempting to do anything. If you try and you are not successful, it simply means you have been given another opportunity to learn more, try again, and be better. Leaders see calamities or challenges as an opportunity to fulfill a purpose, since everything under the sun has a purpose. Leaders also don't wait for opportunities to come their way; they will either chase one or create one. Each and every individual has the ability to create his or her own opportunity.

"If we say, we will enter into the city, then the famine is in the city, and we shall die there: and if we sit here, we die also. Now therefore come, and let us fall unto the host of the Syrians: if they save us alive, we shall live; and if they kill us, we shall but die" (2 Kings 7:4). These are the words of four leprous men who have been condemned by society, but they refused to believe the definition of society for their lives. These men had the thinking, the spirit, and the attitude of leadership. They knew that death was facing them in all choices, but one choice has a possibility of life, so it didn't make sense to them to not do anything because, after all, they had nothing to lose. Death was in the city they were banished from, death was with them in their current status, and death with the possibility of life was also before them when they confronted their fears. These were the derelicts of their society, the nobodies, but they refused to accept the fate society or the culture had handed them and dared to dream of life in the midst of death.

When you read the whole account, you will realize that, due to their fighting attitude, these condemned nobodies brought salvation to the whole of Israel, whereas the somebodies and the learned and the so-called *crème de la crème* were hiding in fear. Death comes only when you make a decision not to live. Any time you decide to defile the destiny of men and pursue the destiny of God for your life, you always live, so death or life is a matter of choice.

As we all know, most great leaders were born out of challenges. For instance, Mandela was born out of the challenges of apartheid in South Africa. Dr. King was born out of the challenges of segregation in the United States. Dr. David Fuseini Abdulai was also born out of the challenge of poverty in northern Ghana in West Africa. Dr. Abdulai, the founder of Shekhinah Clinic, saw a challenge of poverty resulting in sickness and death in the northern part of Ghana. Due to poverty, people couldn't afford medical treatment, so he decided to set up a medical center to provide free medical treatment for the sick and also to provide accommodation for the destitute. Dr. Abdulai saw an opportunity in the problems of the community to serve humanity. Every person born on earth was born to solve a problem by fulfilling the purpose of the problem. This means that if there are seven billion people in the world, there are over seven billion problems in the world for each and every one of those people to fulfill. So do not run away from a problem as it is the opportunity to your success in life. Problems don't come to destroy you, but they come to unearth your success. They also come to take you out of your comfort zone. For you to move to the next stage, you need to move out of your comfort zone. If you want to be successful, go look for problems to solve. If there is nothing in your way, it means you are not moving. If you are moving, then whatever is in your way is meant to be a stepping-stone to your next level. Sometimes what is in your way is meant to be a seat for you to take a break and rethink your strategy. Bear in mind that every problem has a purpose, so find the purpose, and it will no longer be a problem but a catalyst.

Life is not about being born, going to school to get a degree, amassing wealth, getting married, raising a family, and dying just to be buried. There is more to life than just this process. Like God told Jeremiah, before you were formed, He knew you, and before you came out of your mother's womb, He sanctified you. This supports the fact that before you were born, a work had already been assigned to your name. To put it this way, every human embryo has a work assigned to it to be accomplished on earth, so it doesn't matter how the human embryo was formed or who carries it. The conception is the beginning of the fulfillment of purpose, so human abortion goes beyond just the killing of an embryo but also includes a termination of God's purpose. The embryo is infused with the potential to solve a problem to fulfill a specific assignment on earth. At a point in life, the onus is on you to make a choice to identify the potential gifts, develop them, and serve them to the world—or just go through life, die, and allow the gifts to be buried in the cemetery. They remain only *potential* gifts if they are not used to fulfill the assignment. A potential is simply unused talent, so don't let your gift remain a potential, but transform it into service to humanity.

This leads me to the argument that purpose precedes ambitions, and sometimes God will superimpose His purpose on your ambitions, like He did to Mary and Joseph, a young couple who had been engaged and probably had the ambitions of having a big traditional Jewish wedding with great festivities. They probably thought of starting a beautiful life together and owning one of the biggest, if not the biggest, carpentry shops in town. Then comes God offsetting their ambitions with His purpose of making them vessels of the highest honor for accomplishing His purpose of salvation of humanity.

Ambition, according to dictionary.com, is "an earnest desire for some type of achievement or distinction, as power, honor, fame, or wealth, and the willingness to strive for its attainment." The major difference between ambition and purpose is the fact that ambitions are achieved, while purpose is fulfilled. Ambition is *me*-centered: "I have been able to achieve this for me." Ambitions are selfish; they satisfy your ego and pride. They are achieved because you want something, even if it sometimes means trampling over others just to satisfy your ego.

Most times people are confused about ambition and purpose; they might be superficially similar but are really fundamentally different. Achieving your ambitions will bring you satisfaction, which I define as a temporal happiness of an achievement while remaining unsure if that's all there is to your life. Purpose brings you fulfillment, and fulfillment is defined as knowing without a shadow of doubt that you have done what you were born to do. As Apostle Paul said in 2 Timothy 4:6–7, "For I am now ready to be offered, and the time of my departure is at hand. I have fought a good fight, I have finished my course, I have kept the faith." All Paul was saying was that he was ready to die because he had accomplished what he was born to do, and this is fulfillment after accomplishing your purpose.

Ambitions are humans' plans for their lives, but purposes are God's plan for humanity, and His plans for your life supersede your plans since He made you for His plan. Ambition is always how to serve *me* or how to make *me* powerful, while purpose is always how to serve *you* and how to empower *you*.

People become ambitious about their professions not because they want to serve humanity or their communities but because they want to be rich, famous, prestigious, or simply accepted. You may have the ability for your ambitions but will lack the grace that comes with the skill. Ability simply means you are able to do, and being capable means you will be able to do anything you put your mind to, but as to whether you can do it skillfully is another thing. In the case of purpose, you will have both the ability and the gift that come with skill. The ability is the effort and the work you put in to make it happen, and the gift is that which gives your ability the skill, which makes you perform smoothly without any struggles. Don't get this wrong; you need to work on your gift to perfect it, but you don't struggle to execute with perfection. A cheetah might have the ability to swim, but it is gifted to sprint.

When you accomplish your purpose, you will be endowed with the boldness to say, like Paul, that you have finished the race and are ready to die. Those who accomplish their purposes on earth are not scared of death; they are ready to die anytime. Like Jesus said on the cross in John 19:30, "It is finished: and he bowed his head, and gave up the ghost." He had fulfilled his purpose on earth; he was done with the assignment for which he came into the world. It was also said of King David, one of the greatest kings to ever live, that "after he had served his own generation by the will of God, fell on sleep, and was laid unto his fathers, and saw corruption" (Acts 3:36).

This is a little story on purpose in life—it is like the whole world is engaged in a jigsaw puzzle, and every one born on earth has a piece of the puzzle given to him or her in the womb. So your whole purpose in life is to drive to where the jigsaw puzzle is and place your piece in its right spot. The moment you were born, you started your journey toward the jigsaw puzzle to go place your piece in its right spot, and the moment you place your piece, you are done, and then you leave the world. Just like anybody embarking on a journey with a vehicle built by an auto mechanic, in this case your parents are the mechanics who use tools like values, ethics, principles, traditions, and culture to build you a vehicle for the journey of life, and this is something you don't have control, or have very limited control, over. This is a very important part of life because you need a very good vehicle to embark on the journey, and all that goes into your upbringing becomes the materials used for the vehicle.

The time needed for the making of the vehicle as well as the wisdom and the knowledge of the mechanic are very vital. The durability of the vehicle to withstand the terrain—the hills, mountains, valleys, potholes, manholes, rain, sunshine, mud, gravels, and sand—of life will be determined by the materials used in building the vehicle. If you have good mechanics who are knowledgeable about the harshness of the terrain, they will use solid metals and take their time in molding the vehicle to withstand the shocks, the bumps, and the kicks. Unfortunately for others, they don't have good mechanics, or they bounce from one busy mechanic to the other and at a point have to complete the vehicles themselves. In this case I am referring to those who either don't have parents or have troubled parents or teenage parents, or who live in foster homes and sometimes raise themselves. We still have to embark on this journey of life anyway; we have no option, but that is why we are all obliged to pull over for a broken vehicle by the roadside to assist the driver in fixing it so he or she can keep moving. All I am saying is that the onus is on the privileged ones to help the disadvantaged ones in this journey of life.

When you reach the age of maturity, the vehicle is handed over to you to fuel it with gas. This time you have absolute control over which gas to put in the car and whether you fill the whole tank or you keep filling the tank a little bit at a time as you go along—this is all within your control. Mind you, some cars have to use premium fuel based on the make of the car. At this stage, it is the knowledge you acquire. Remember that the longer you stay at the gas station to fill up your tank, the longer the distance you can cover before running out of gas. Premium gas is the finest quality, so it is important you acquire good information and not fill your vehicle with any junk, which will cause your vehicle to break down along the way.

The quality of gas in your vehicle will determine the performance of the vehicle. This means that the quality of information with which you feed yourself is vital to your performance in life. After the vehicle is maintained and fueled, you set off to go place your puzzle in its right spot. On your way in the journey of life, you may choose to drive alone or pick up a codriver—that is up to you.

When you set off either alone or with a codriver, your decision to stop at every rest stop and how long to rest, as well as the exits you take, will get you to your destination either sooner or later, and these are the choices you make in life.

Unfortunately, others give up on their way due to vehicle breakdowns as a result of bumps, kicks, or other blows in life. Sometimes others give up due to shortage of gas (lack of knowledge), wrong exits due to bad advice (check the company of friends you keep), or even detours (like teenage childbirth).

In this journey you can achieve your ambitions by showing off your ability to drive by negotiating sharp turns at a high speed or bouncing your vehicle around to get you fame and attention, which is all about you. You can also make this journey a fulfilled one by stopping to give a helping hand to those with broken vehicles or help give directions to lost travelers, which will be service to humanity and not about you. The danger in achieving your ambitions is that you might be caught up in the "all about me syndrome" and lose focus on getting to the jigsaw puzzle to place your piece in its rightful place, which is the most important thing in life. Ambitions make you chase after power, wealth, fame, and attainment at the expense of serving humanity. It is only when you place your piece in its rightful place on the jigsaw puzzle will you be able to say "It is finished, I have served my generation, and I can now rest in peace with my fathers."

Many people find themselves at the crossroads of ambition and purpose, and they get confused as to what choice to make. If you ever find yourself in this dilemma, which is normal in this journey of life, ask yourself these questions, and your honest answers should influence your decision: (1) Is this about me, or is it about service to humanity? (2) Is this going to bring me fulfillment at the end of the day?

To establish the difference between a leader and a manager, let us first define a manager, and this is my definition: a supervisor within the administrative hierarchy as a custodian who is to maintain and utilize that which has been entrusted to his or her care for the maximization of profit or the achievement of a certain goal. So managers are motivated by the achievement of the goal, no matter what the cost is. Managers coordinate resources for the achievement of a goal, but leaders *cultivate* and coordinate resources for the achievement of a goal. This is the reason it takes leaders a longer time to achieve their goals, because if the resources are not available, leaders will devote time to cultivate them for their use. It is the same reason leaders don't easily fire people, because they believe in people.

Managers only know how to coordinate and don't cultivate, so they can easily fire people and hire replacements in a heartbeat. Leaders do not get rid of an employee based on performance. Rather, the leader sees the employee's performance issue as his or her inability to live up to his or her leadership expectations. The leader believes that no matter what the issues of the employee are, he or she as a leader should and must be able to get to the core of it and bring a transformation. Managers tell you what to do, but leaders will show you how to do it. In a nutshell, leaders create the path, and managers maintain it. Leaders always venture into the unknown and are not scared of making mistakes, for mistakes are part of the unknown. A successful business needs a blend of good leaders and good managers. The leaders set the target or vision for the company, and managers make sure the targets are achieved.

Managers will take the time to explain to you what needs to be done; they are skillful in teaching by instructions, while leaders will take the time to come and do it with you, so you can learn not just by knowing what to do but also how to do it. As one of the great leaders in the Bible, Apostle Paul, wrote in Philippians 4:9, "Those things, which ye have both learned, and received, and heard, and seen in me, do: and the God of peace shall be with you." This shows that Paul was not just telling the disciples what to do, but he was demonstrating it in his lifestyle as well.

Leaders will always want to get to the root cause of a problem to deal with it from there. In other words, when you make a mistake, leaders don't quickly jump to disciplinary actions but will want to get into your personal life to find out if there is something they can help you fix. Managers, however, will resort to disciplinary action, and they don't believe in letting your personal life affect your output on the job.

Leaders always take pleasure in seeing growth in your personal life, because they believe you can always perform better professionally when you have a sound personal life. Therefore, they tend to advocate for more pay and more incentives like good insurance and more personal and vacation hours for their employees.

Managers will always want to uphold the rules and will not bend them for anything because they have a goal to achieve, but when leaders uphold the rules it is because they want to build in you a character. For managers, meeting the goal is personal because they measure their growth by that; it tells them how well they have been able to manage. For a leader, meeting the goal is collective; it tells them how the team has grown. So to the leader, it's a measuring tool for team growth. Most importantly it tells the leader how individuals in the team have developed to collectively hit the goal; the achievement of the said goal is the least of the leader's priorities. Leaders see the achievement of the goal from this perspective, first as a measuring tool for individual growth in the team, which has secondly affected the growth of the team, which has thirdly influenced the achievement of the goal.

For the manager, it is seen in reverse. The manager's priority is the goal because it is an indication of the manager's growth as the team captain, which has resulted in the team growth, which has affected the individual growth. To the manager, the individual has grown because the manager devised a good strategy for the team and has influenced the growth of the individual. Managers believe the success of the team depends on the managers themselves, whereas leaders believe the success of the team depends on each individual team member. Managers are quick to pat themselves on the back, but leaders always give glory to the team; they take themselves out of the glory. Leaders are also quick to take the blame for the team's failure, whereas managers quickly blame the team for failure and take themselves out of failure.

Because leaders believe the success of the team depends on strong individuals, they are always interested in building personal relationships with the individuals, whereas managers don't really bother about personal relationships with the individuals on the team; they care only about professional relationships with team members.

Leaders don't mind making decisions that are out of the norm, and if it doesn't work, they take the heat, but managers don't want to be blamed, so they always abide by the norm.

Finally, leaders don't believe in the permanence of the team; in other words, they always want to grow the team to move up either in the company or to move on in their lives. Leaders are also not scared of their subordinates, or anybody for that matter, and take their positions because they don't measure their value by their titles but by the influence they make on the people around them.

A developed leader can no longer be a manager. The moment you develop your leadership gift to a certain level, it will be nearly impossible for you to operate in a manager's position. To the leader, the only difference between the leader and the subordinate is the level of the administrative hierarchy, but in terms of the value of their work, they are the same. Managers also believe that the difference between them and the subordinate is their level of the administrative hierarchy, but their level of work is seen as more valuable than their subordinate's.

Leadership is an essential institution in the development of the human institution; without it, humanity would be in chaos. As the saying goes, when the blind lead the blind, they both fall into a pit. Unfortunately, the leadership office has been misused as a weapon of mass destruction, with some people hiding behind heinous and cynical ideas in the guise of leadership to destroy humanity. This is largely because we sometimes make a mistake by placing wrong leadership in the wrong office, and that becomes very dangerous.

In this section we are going to take a look at the two ratings of leadership in view of the definitions given so far for ambition and purpose—we will look at purposeful leadership and ambitious leadership. There is a very slippery slope between these two ratings that has eluded most good purposeful leaders, causing them to slip into being ambitious leaders. In this context, we will discuss some examples of purposeful leaders and some ambitious leaders.

Purposeful leadership always exhibits wisdom and understanding that result in good judgment and a clear focus on the assignment. The assignment will always keep you in check, and if your assignment is not contaminated with ambition, you will always make the right choice.

Before we continue, let us take a look at the definition of these two powerful words: wisdom and understanding.

Wisdom, they say, is the application of knowledge, but I say wisdom is the rightful application of good knowledge. For example, your dad asks you to clean the house before he gets back home from work, but you decide to start by cleaning your bedroom, and just as you are about to clean the living room, your father shows up with visitors to find the living room still dirty. He is not going to be happy with you. First of all, he gave you good knowledge—that is, clean the house—and you applied the good knowledge, but you didn't apply it correctly, because you didn't dig into the roots of the good knowledge to understand how you were supposed to apply the good knowledge rightly. You see, if you always ask for the *why*, the *how* becomes easy, and the *why* gives you an understanding. So, in this case, the wrongful application of the good knowledge did not result in wisdom but rather in folly.

Understanding is a vital component of wisdom, and as the scripture says, "With all your getting get understanding" (Prov. 4:7). I will define understanding in the literal sense of the word by breaking it into two. The prefix "under" means "beneath" or "roots," and "stand" is an upright position or posture, so to get a better picture of an idea or an action, you need to stand upright in its very roots to see where it is springing out from. So understanding simply means taking a position at the roots; knowing the foundation of a thing gives you a better position, or a better stand, which will make you deal with that thing more wisely. In other words, understanding is literally standing under a thing so you see the roots, which is the foundation, or the intent or the reason, and that puts you in a better position to deal with it. That is why Proverbs 4:7 says, "Wisdom is the principal thing; therefore, get wisdom: and with all thy getting get understanding." The two most powerful keys to success in life are wisdom and understanding, and if you possess these two attributes, there is no way you will not be successful.

The phrase "life is not fair" is not the truth, but rather life is the fairest institution ever established for man. "I returned, and saw under the sun, that the race is not to the swift, nor the battle to the strong, neither yet bread to the wise, nor yet riches to men of understanding, nor yet favour to men of skill; but time and chance happeneth to them all" (Eccles. 9:11). This means that life owes nobody anything but time and chance. Chance here means the opportunity for change, so all life owes anybody on earth is time and the opportunity for change.

Time and change happen to everybody born on earth. Everybody has access to twenty-four hours a day; nobody has more, and nobody has less. Everybody experiences winter, spring, summer, and fall. In the same way, the opportunity for change happens to everybody. Everybody goes through the changes of life, from sperm to fetus to baby to youth to adult. The problem here is what we do with the time and the opportunity for change that come our way every day. If you misuse them, you will end up believing the lie that life is not fair. If you are diligent with time and the opportunity for change, you will realize that indeed life is very fair. Your current situation might be influenced by either your parents or somebody who has some level of influence over your life, but the good news is that you have the ability to accept it or change it.

Remember the three most important elements of leadership: gift, service to humanity, and self-fulfillment. These happen to be the measurement for leadership; therefore, any leadership that falls short of these will be on a slippery slope to ambitious leadership.

One example of an ambitious leader who began as a purposeful leader is Osagyefo Dr. Kwame Nkrumah of Ghana, West Africa. He led Ghana to independence and became its first president. Dr. Nkrumah was gifted in his field of work. He was an eloquent speaker and a great thinker, and he was selfless for the most part in the execution of leadership in the service of humanity. Some decisions he made, however, had others question his service for humanity in light of his autocratic regime in 1964.

Most of Dr. Nkrumah's mistakes were a result of his African Unity vision. In pursuit of this vision, he sacrificed Ghana's democracy and its liberty as he realized he was a lone ranger in this vision. Dr. Nkrumah sought to unite the African continent for Africans to live in peace, harmony, and prosperity without any oppression. He was caught in a dilemma when he realized that none of the independent African heads of state were seeing the same vision of a United States of Africa. This was a vision he believed could be achieved only with political power, and so he needed to entrench himself in power to enable him to fulfill this vision. He needed the power as the president of Ghana to propagate the African Unity agenda, so in this process, he had to suppress all opposition to his presidency, and this resulted in some human rights violations.

No matter how passionate you find yourself about your dream, you must make sure that every decision you make in that pursuit is fulfilling all three elements of leadership:

1. Do you have the gift?
2. Does it serve humanity?
3. Will it fulfill you at the end of the day?

Most times you have to understand your role and don't force yourself to do that which has been assigned to another generation, as it happened in 2 Samuel 7: "That the king said unto Nathan the prophet, see now I dwell in an house of cedar, but the ark of God dwelleth within curtains" (2 Sam. 7:2). "And when thy days be fulfilled, and thou shalt sleep with thy fathers, I will set up thy seed after thee, which shall proceed out of thy bowels, and I will establish his kingdom. He shall build a house for my name, and I will establish the throne of his kingdom forever" (2 Sam. 7:12–13). King David, one of the greatest leaders the world has ever known, wanted to build a temple for God, but God told him, "No, you were called to fight; that is your purpose, and you are doing just fine." He had prepared David's son, which was the generation after him, to do the building for Him.

Sometimes your assignment is just to lay the foundation by preparing the next generation to do the building, and if you are not careful, ambition will tell you to do the building as well for people to know that you started it and you have completed it. If you don't listen to purpose and you decide to listen to ambition, you will make a mess of all the good you have done. In the same light, Jesus came into the world and prepared twelve men, out of which one betrayed him, and after that He said, "It is finished." He empowered them to continue His assignment.

I strongly believe that if Dr. Nkrumah had found about ten African leaders at that time to be as passionate, insightful, and enthusiastic as he was about the African Unity dream, he probably wouldn't have entrenched himself in power. His dream of African Unity was never selfish, and his ambition may have stemmed from fear of the dream not being realized after seeing the passive attitude of his peers. It was clear that Dr. Nkrumah was generations ahead of his contemporaries, and they were not seeing what he was seeing, and that can be very frustrating. He could have taken another route by mentoring, grooming, and imbibing the vision into a new breed of leaders to take over the vision from him. Probably his assignment was to lay the foundation by preparing the mind-set and grooming the next generation to fulfill the noble vision for the continent.

Taking into consideration the people who had just come out of colonial bondage, with their confidence invested into another race other than themselves and with a subservient mentality and attitude, it would be very difficult to build a progressive nation or continent.

Dr. Nkrumah became ambitious when he was faced with the reality that the African leaders at that time were not seeing what he was seeing and that the moment he left the scene, the African Unity dream would not be fulfilled because it would be leaving with him. When frustration set in, he became ambitious and decided to get it done by any means necessary, thinking that after all, the end would justify the means. This is the language of ambition, and purposeful leaders must refrain from it. So even though Dr. Nkrumah had a noble vision, he allowed ambition to take a better part of his service to humanity, and this led him to make certain choices that resulted in the death and the pain of his own people.

Nelson Mandela, by contrast, broke the wings of apartheid, hate, and oppression to liberate his people from tyranny. Mandela was one leader who could have easily slipped into ambitious leadership, but he knew exactly what his assignment was and did just that, and that is the reason he is deemed one of the greatest leaders the world has ever known.

Mandela could have easily been a lifetime president of South Africa, but he chose to teach South Africa, and for that matter, the world, a lesson that the progress of humanity is more important than his ambitions, and he made his principles clear in this statement: "During my lifetime, I have dedicated myself to this struggle of the African people. I have fought against white domination, and I have fought against black domination. I have cherished the ideal of a democratic and free society in which all persons live together in harmony and with equal opportunities. It is an ideal which I hope to live for and to achieve. But if needs be, it is an ideal for which I am prepared to die."

He also exhibited to the world that the foundation of leadership is love when he said, "As I walked out the door toward the gate that would lead to my freedom, I knew if I didn't leave my bitterness and hatred behind, I'd still be in prison."

So, if your leadership is causing loss of purpose, loss of lives, fear, and pain to the very people you are supposed to serve, then you need to question your choices. Mandela spent about a third of his life in jail and had every reason to be bitter, and yet he had not an iota of hate in him. He knew that his expression of hate could set the whole country ablaze, which would result in loss of purpose and lives as well as unleash pain on the lives of the people he had fought so hard to liberate.

I am convinced Nelson Mandela knew his purpose was to break down the tall, thick walls of apartheid and hate not only in the laws of the land but also in the hearts of humanity. He did not only liberate black South Africa but also liberated the oppressors as well of their hate for humanity. He also understood that the success of his leadership was not measured by how long he stayed in office but in how ready he prepared a successor. He knew he was done with his assignment in life, and not wanting to taint his image by being ambitious, after placing his puzzle piece in its rightful spot, he left the scene. He has now become an icon, an example and an epitome of purposeful leadership to the entire world and to generations yet to come.

Finally, we cannot talk about purposeful leadership without mentioning Rev. Dr. Martin Luther King Jr., a man who became the conscience of his generation. Purposeful leadership must always appeal to the conscience of humanity, and Dr. King knew that the ultimate price of this type of leadership was his life.

In light of the leadership definitions given so far, there are some world figures who don't even qualify for the title of *bad* leadership—such as Adolf Hitler, Joseph Stalin, Kim Jong-Un, Kim Jong-Il, Idi Amin, Osama Bin-Laden, and the like. They are all frustrated individuals who don't know what to do with their lives and can be classified only as dictators. The likes of these world figures obviously don't understand leadership or the role they seek to operate in. Their conduct supports the argument that leadership is not about amassing followers, neither is leadership charisma nor a title, since they possess all these qualities but lack the character and substance of leadership. They may have a gift but not selfless service of humanity, and definitely not a sense of fulfillment at the end of the day.

ach and every individual born on earth happens to be within one of these stages of leadership at any point in time. This gives credence to the fact that everybody was born with a leadership gift, and there are no exceptions.

Developed Leadership Stage: This is the ultimate stage of leadership gift, which has been identified, developed, and is serving humanity. This is the stage in which one has maximum influence in his or her area of gifting.

Developing Leadership Stage: This is the stage in which one has identified the gift and is in the process of developing it, either through formal or informal training to sharpen the skill. Most people get derailed at this stage, due to lack of proper guidance and misunderstanding of the concept of leadership. This influences them to take what seems to be the more financially rewarding option.

Potential Leadership Stage: This is the stage in which most people are probing and searching to find themselves in life. This is also the stage in which the majority of people are trapped and believe they were born only to follow and don't have any leadership gift.

Leadership Is Not Rulership over People

eadership has always been confused with rulership over people, and this has created mayhem in the world. In Genesis 1:26, God said, "Let us make man in our image, after our likeness: and let them have dominion over the fish of the sea, and over the fowl of the air, and over the cattle and over all the earth, and over every creeping thing that creepeth upon the earth." In this statement of intent made by the Creator, He never mentioned anywhere to let them have dominion over one another. In other words, He never mentioned that man would have dominion over another man. Bear in mind that God created man for leadership. The whole purpose of man was to be a leader and ruler in life, so if leadership included rulership over another man, God would have stated it right then when He was talking about the leadership of man.

Rulership over man means ownership, which leads to worship, and that is the preserve of God, the maker of man, because you can rule over only what you make. Therefore, rulership of man over another man is a violation of God's purpose. Rulership over man by man was orchestrated by man to fulfill his own selfish ambitions.

When God created man, He had a kingdom in mind, as Jesus stated in the Lord's Prayer. God intended to extend His domain of rulership to earth. God intended to rule over man, His creation, while man ruled over the earth, and at the same time He intended to make man a cocreator. Remember, you can rule over only what you make or own, so that was why God asked Adam to name the animals. It wasn't because God couldn't name them Himself, but He wanted Adam to feel a part of creation so he would have that mandate and authority to rule over it.

Just to make this point clear, God never set up any kingdom on earth; the kingdoms of rulership is man's institution.

God's system of rulership He set up with the people of Israel was a system of colony. That was why the people of Israel never had kings, but prophets, who were just custodians and were only administering God's laws. That is, the prophets were only administrative leaders; they were not making the laws, but God, who was their ruler, was making the laws for the prophets to administer. So, even when God gave in to the demands of the people of Israel and allowed them to have kings, God was still the ruler. All the kings of Israel who did the right things were governing by the laws of God through the prophets. Realize that any time God is involved in the process of choosing the king, He does it based on the gifts of that person to fulfill His purpose.

Throughout the nation of Israel, they had no kings but only judges and elders, until 1 Samuel 8:4–5, and this was God's response in 1 Samuel 8:7: "Hearken unto the voice of the people in all that they say unto thee: for they have not rejected thee, but they have rejected me, that I should not rule over them." This expresses God's displeasure over the nation's request for a king because they were seeking to violate His purpose.

Gideon understood this better after he caught the revelation in Judges 8:22–23: "Then the men of Israel said unto Gideon, rule thou over us, both thou, and thy son, and thy son's son also: for thou hast delivered us from the hand of the Midian. And Gideon said unto them, I will not rule over you, neither shall my son rule over you: The Lord shall rule over you."

Man's kingdom of rulership was a replica of God's, but that of man is illegitimate because man is ruling over what he did not make. In a kingdom of rulership, rulership is by decree, according to the pleasure of the king and not by general consensus because the king is the ultimate, and all others are subjects. So you can imagine a wicked man with wicked desires will make only wicked laws to suppress the subjects.

That is why God chose David for the people of Israel, because he was an upright man, and God knew the enormous power and authority vested in a king, so putting a man in such a position, he ought to be an upright man. If you look at the history of Israel, any time the people of Israel pick a king, it ends up being disastrous, but any time God picks one for them, it's always a success.

The word "subjects" can be broken into two—the prefix "sub" means "under" or "inferior," and "jects" is a Latin root word meaning "throw," and you can throw only an object. So "subjects" means "inferior objects" to humans (the king), and that is why the king can do unto any of his subjects anything according to his pleasure or will, because they are not considered humans but objects. In Matthew 6:9–13, when Jesus was teaching the disciples the manner in which they ought to pray, He said, "Thy kingdom come. Thy will be done in earth, as it is in heaven." This gives you an idea of a colony, where God's will in His heavenly kingdom will be done here on earth. In a colony, the king rules over his people in one country from another country. One may ask, what is the will of God for man? In John 6:38 Jesus said, "For I came down from heaven, not to do mine own will, but the will of him that sent me." And in John 10:10, again He said He came that we might have life and that we might have it more abundantly. So the will of God is for us to live the life He created us to live, and that being a subject does not give you the liberty and right to live the life you were born to live.

This is why kingdoms of rulership and all other systems that seek to rule over mankind is failing, because they are in violation of God's purpose for mankind. Democracy is thriving in our world today not because it is the US agenda but because it is the only system, even with its flaws, that sees the right to live the life you were born to live as sacred. You see, democracy is not the western world's way of governance, but rather, humanity's way of governance. Democracy begins the very moment we recognize the sacredness of one's existence. The point is that in the DNA of mankind is rulership, and you cannot rule over a ruler and expect peace; there will always be rebellion. Every man has to fight to subdue his pride any time he is willingly or unwillingly submitting to another man's control.

To rule over other rulers, you first have to break their spirits and self-esteem by feeding their minds with wrong information about their inferiority and your superiority. You must succeed in bringing them to a level at which they see their very existence as dependent on you. In effect, you have to enslave them mentally to become subservient to you to rule over them. The day they realize who they are marks the beginning of a revolt, and the wars and chaos in the history of the world can be traced to one and only one thing, which is the struggle for power over man by another man. Man by nature is wired to rule, and you cannot rule over another and expect peace or an absence of war.

Leadership, as it has been stated in this book as related to power, control, charisma, and so on, works only in the animal kingdom because animals are not reasoning beings; they operate on instincts. The animal kingdom, therefore, resorts to power, control, and charisma to protect its territories and families.

This is why kingdoms of rulership were always fighting. When the British understood this concept, for example, the kingdom decided to step back and let democracy run the country. The collapse of powerful kingdoms of rulership in the world is an indication of the fact that rulership over mankind is not in harmony with the spirit of man. As it is recorded in Ecclesiastes 8:9, "All this I have seen, and applied my heart to every work that is done under the sun: There is a time in which one man rules over another to his own hurt." In this verse, the writer is bringing home the point that when a man rules over another man, he would resist it one day when he realizes his full potential. Any system of governance that does not uphold the sacredness of humanity is in violation of God's purpose. Since rulership is based on ownership, rulership does not adhere to any law, but that which will bring pleasure to the ruler.

Most often we make a mistake in thinking that governance is the same as rulership. According to dictionary.com, ruling is "an authoritative decision, as one by a judge on a debated point of law," or the act of "governing or dominating, controlling or predominating."

Rulership is about control and domination, which results in worship and is motivated by ownership; you cannot rule over something you don't own. Governance is an administrative hierarchy that coordinates the various components of an institution for the advancement of a community. Rulership is synonymous with kingdoms of rulership, whereas governance is synonymous with democracy. Kingdoms rule because in a kingdom of rulership, it is about ownership, but democracy governs. The seed of pride and man wanting to play God was introduced in the garden when the serpent influenced man to disobey God. That was when man decided to rule and be worshipped like God.

God never gave sovereignty of man by man to any human; He is the only sovereign being, and therefore no human being is sovereign. Man can govern only another man, but rulership over man is the preserve of the one and only sovereign entity, God Almighty.

God never set up a system of rulership for the people of Israel but rather an administrative system of governance. When God sent Moses to deliver the people of Israel, in the entire Exodus 3, when God was talking to Moses about the children of Israel, He kept referring to the children of Israel as His people. God knew that Moses was going to lead them, but He never gave Moses sovereignty over the children of Israel. God emphasized "my people" to establish His sovereignty over the people of Israel. "Come now therefore, and I will send thee unto Pharaoh, that thou mayest bring forth my people the children of Israel out of Egypt" (Exod. 3:10). In Exodus 34, God gave Moses His rules to go and govern the children of Israel. Rulers are sovereign; therefore, they rule by their own laws and not the laws of another sovereignty.

Leadership has nothing to do with sovereignty or an office, but rather all leadership is a gift, and administration identifies leadership gifts to run the institutional hierarchy. Governance is an administrative system that has been assigned roles, based on the structure of hierarchy. Therefore, gifts are assigned roles within the system of administration to govern.

6

Classification of Leadership

Leadership is a very complex and dynamic institution whose definition is within its context of operation; like beauty, it is defined in a context. Leadership might be superficially different in areas of operation, but its fundamental principles are the same. Leadership governs every aspect of humanity—from home, school, and work to places of worship and politics, you name it—and humanity cannot function without leadership. Leadership brings vision, focus, order, direction, and harmony to society, which results in progress and beauty.

There might be various leadership styles, like the transformational leadership, democratic leadership, and autocratic leadership, but there are only two classifications of leadership: corporate leadership and servant leadership. Corporate leadership is synonymous with ambitious leadership, whereas servant leadership is to purposeful leadership.

Motivated by power, profit, and ownership, institutions like kingdoms of rulership, companies, and autocratic government, and so on all fall under the category of corporate leadership. This is the traditional concept of leadership that was first introduced to the world by the ancient Greek philosophers who got caught up like a wildfire. This concept was propagated by the world's influential monarchs, the British and the Romans, to create a system of subservient people for them to rule over. It is more likely to see definitions given in the dictionaries linked to this concept.

One classic example of corporate leadership is the kingdoms of rulership wherein a king is deemed as the owner of the land and the people. The Zulu kingdom, for example, observes a first fruit practice, and that is every first fruit harvested at the beginning of every harvest season from the Zulu lands is taken to the king to eat first before anybody else in the kingdom can taste it. This signifies ownership of the land and the people; in other words, the land is of the king, and his subjects are farming on his land so he has to be satisfied first before anybody else.

Another example of ownership can be seen in the Asante kingdom in Ghana. When the king is dancing during ceremonies, he throws both hands up and embraces himself. This signifies that the land and the people in it belong to the king. Again, during the British colonization of the world, colonies were paying taxes to the Queen of England from all over the world. In that same manner, for companies to be able to operate profitably and successfully, the management of the company is taught to develop a sense of ownership. This creates within the subconscious an attitude to make a profit for yourself. Even though it is profit for the company, it feels like it is for you because of the sense of ownership. The company ownership concept is for the purpose of making a profit for the company and nothing else.

Power is a major characteristic of corporate leadership, and we all know how powerful companies or business institutions get when they amass wealth. They pursue the wealth to the point that it goes beyond just making a profit to being powerful enough to influence policies. One example is oil companies that are polluting the environment and yet no one seems to do anything about it, because the companies have the power to shut up all opposition. Also, the kings have so much power, their word becomes law, and people may disagree with them but may not be able to do anything about it.

Charisma is also an essential characteristic of corporate leadership, so kings are trained and prepared to be equipped for the office of a king. Business institutions sometimes scout for charismatic managers to invest in them for top management positions. Charisma is cherished in corporate leadership so much that all other qualities are often overlooked to the point that people are convinced that charisma is all it takes to be a leader. Charisma has the power to hypnotize its audience and transport the people into a trancelike state so that they don't question the character or the motive behind it. Charisma is also the easiest and the quickest way to draw attention and audience, and it's a dangerous tool in the hands of a dictator. As we all know, the world has been led into destruction by certain charismatic figures.

Office or title is the next essential characteristic of corporate leadership. As a matter of fact, it is so essential that without it one cannot function in corporate leadership. That is why people don't mind doing anything, including manipulation and bribery or even killing, to obtain an office or a title.

Numbers and control are the last elements of corporate leadership. The bigger the number of people you control, the more effective or powerful you are in corporate leadership. This is why corporate leaders are always striving hard to influence and amass a large following to expand their area of control and power.

Note that all these characteristics of corporate leadership are interdependent in the achievement of the bigger goal.

These characteristics are the most powerful and influential features that seem to influence the definitions of leadership, and these characteristics also differentiate corporate leadership from service leadership.

Corporate leadership will do anything to advance its cause, because it is of the opinion that its position is by divine providence.

This kind of leadership is motivated by what we call the three Ps: purpose, people, and progress. Service leadership is a selfless act of purpose to serve people to bring about progress to humanity. Community service, religious bodies, true democratic governments, and so on fall under service leadership. This is the subtlest leadership definition you'll ever find in the dictionaries. Service leadership does not require any of the characteristics of corporate leadership listed earlier to function, but they both share some common principles of planning, determination, visions, goals, commitment, passionate pursuit, and many more.

Service leadership does not require power or ownership to operate. As a matter of fact, most service leaders don't possess either of these. Service leadership also does not require charisma to operate; instead it requires character. No office or title is needed. All that is required is self-worth and self-discovery with a determination to lead your generation with your gifts.

Service leadership is not motivated by profit, power, or ownership but instead by fulfillment of purpose in the service of humanity, and anybody born on planet Earth has the potential and the gifts to become a service leader. Service leadership is and always will be a tool for development and advancement of humanity in our world, whereas corporate leadership has been a tool to inflict pain and anguish on humanity. However, this is not to say that corporate leadership has not been or cannot be an influence in the development of humanity; the caution is that it is a very slippery slope, and if ultimate care is not taken, it becomes a tool for destruction, especially in the hands of the wicked.

One major institution under service leadership that has the capacity to positively affect humanity, but has lost its credibility, is democratic governance. There is the notion that politics is a dirty game, which unfortunately has been accepted, so honest and upright leaders are shunning this field of leadership. The problem is that we define politics by the office, instead of the gift of running the office. So we keep voting for politicians instead of the right leadership gift to run the office. The point here is that the more that good leaders stay away from democratic politics, the more it's been muddied by dirty people. To politicians, leadership is a profession, and they may not have the right leadership gift to run that office. How can an institution so strategic and so very essential in the service and advancement of humanity be left in the hands of dirty people? What politics needs now are good leaders who are dedicated to the development and service of humanity.

7

The Principles of a Good Leader

Good leadership principles are acquired through learning and the discipline to practice them. Just like any entity, leadership operates on certain principles, and for you to be successful, you need to adopt these principles. As you learn or acquire the information, you transform the knowledge into principles to guide your life. Life without principles is like a boat without a captain; it goes wayward and eventually gets destroyed by storms or any form of adversity. This understanding is derived from Psalm 119:105: "Thy word is a lamp unto my feet, and a light unto my path." In other words, the word of God is available to all, which is the information representing the light of God for humanity. So out of God's light, you can draw some light for your lamp, representing principles to guide your life, and out of those principles based on the word of God, your path of life becomes illuminated with knowledge, understanding, and wisdom.

Principles are intrinsic values of the gift, based on a fundamental truth you are convinced of, which influences your attitude in life. First of all, those values must be based on a fundamental truth, which is the word of God, and you must be convinced about the truth that when you live your life by it, you will always be on the right path, and then it will influence your attitude. Leadership is a lifestyle; therefore, every lifestyle is built on principles. Principles are like the very breath of an entity, and without them an entity is lifeless.

Excellence is one of the most essential values that define leadership; it is the ultimate fruit of leadership. Excellence is simply being the best of you and going beyond the expectations society has set for you. It is born out of the spirit of perfection man is made of, and so we don't work hard to excel; we have only to desire it because it is within our DNA. This is why sometimes you do something spectacular and everybody is amazed and yet you are not satisfied, so you tell yourself that you want to go beyond that. You are constantly competing not with any other person but yourself, because nobody knows your purpose, vision, or dreams better than you. The principle of excellence compels you to compete with yourself; it makes you set the record and break it yourself. It gives you the attitude to grow beyond your weaknesses, which always makes you move the finish line further. Man is an expression of God's excellence, so excellence is in the DNA of man, and all we need to do is to unearth that attribute.

Understanding the Principle
of Time Management

Time and change are two inevitable essentials beyond the control of mankind but are within mankind's management. In other words, whether we are ready or not, time is ticking; it is moving on, waiting for no one, and whether we are ready or not, change is happening to us and around us, and it is not within our power to stop either of them. Change here is the opportunity to grow.

God made it to be fair to all humanity so that nobody has the advantage of controlling time and change to his or her favor, and that also gives nobody the excuse for not having enough time or change in life. The same twenty-four hours is available to all; we cannot stop time, neither can we extend or shorten time. We have to be judicious about the use of our time. We need to invest our time and not spend it. If we invest, it yields returns, but if we spend, we are not going to get anything back. Meaning, we need to invest our time into things that will be beneficial to our success in life. Remember that time spent can never be retrieved, but time invested either in our lives or the lives of other people will always be fruitful.

In God's infinite wisdom, He grouped time into hours, days, weeks, months, seasons, and years for our proper management and use. The good thing about that is that we will have the opportunity to redeem the time; in other words, when you miss it yesterday, you can have another opportunity today, and today can also give you the opportunity to prepare for tomorrow, and just in case you miss today, you can have another shot tomorrow. Time has also been rolled into seasons, so if you miss it in one season, it is not over; another season is coming.

To be a good leader, you must understand time and the seasons, and you have to put every tick of the clock to good use. You must invest time into your change, and it will always lead you to your purpose in life. Change will happen one way or the other, and the only way it will be to your advantage is when you have prepared yourself by putting every second of your time to good use.

For your information, change is always uncomfortable, and it comes with the unknown for growth, so you always have to learn new things and challenges to benefit from change. So then you have to understand that challenges are not meant to break you but rather to make you into what you were born to be. A classic example is a crawling child who is growing to walk. The child must learn to walk, which is new or unknown to the child, with all the challenges of tripping and falling. The child will always rise up and fall again. In other words, without falling and rising, the child can never walk, so the fear of falling does not stop the child from rising up and trying again. You can never experience growth if you don't adapt to change, and change comes with falling and rising; if you are not falling in your life, it means you are not adapting to change, and if you are not adapting to change, then it means you are not growing.

Change also brings movement or progression, so if you are not adapting to change, it means you are not progressing, but you will still be moving from bad to worse. There is no stagnant position in life; you are either moving forward or you are moving backward. Do you know that your success in life depends on how many times you fall, meaning the more you fall, the closer you are to success? Remember the crawling child? The more the child falls and rises, the better the child gets at walking.

The more you understand the management of time, the smoother your transition to change, so change does not hit you as unexpectedly. Good time management gives you the space to prepare for change. Remember that there is no wrong time in doing the right thing. It is always the right time to do the right thing in life.

Vision is the ability to see with your mind; vision is not the function of the eye, but of the mind. Here is a short story of two laborers digging a foundation for a building: The first laborer was asked by a passerby, "What are you doing my friend?" And the first laborer's response was, "We are digging a foundation." Then he asked the second laborer, "What are you doing my friend?" And the second laborer's response was, "We are building a six-classroom block for the community to help educate the youth." This tells you that the second laborer has a vision of the end result of what they have just begun, which is a six-classroom block to educate the youth. The building is not completed for the eyes to see, but he has already seen it with his mind. The first laborer saw only what he was doing because he was relating to his eyesight.

To be a good leader, you must cultivate the principle of always capturing the image of your destination in your mind, and that is called *vision*. If you have the image of your destination in mind, it gives you an idea of what your destination is like. Any time you are embarking on anything, you must always learn to see the end of the thing in mind; in other words, have a mental picture of the thing in mind before you begin. This is very important because one of the first things the excitement of the mental image does is to eliminate procrastination and set you up to hit the road.

Do not confuse desire with vision, for those who procrastinate only desire, but they don't cultivate the principle of capturing the image in their minds, because those who add vision to desire don't procrastinate. Your desire must always feed on what you see in your mind, and that will drive you to move. People who procrastinate feed their desires with what they see others do and not on what they see in their minds. Your desire must always see to move you, so if it's always seeing what's in your mind, you are always on the move, but if it sees what others do, then you cannot move when those people are not around.

Second, since vision eliminates any delays on your part, you can invest your resources into anything that will get you to your destination faster. Since it motivates you to plan, you pay attention to every detail of your life and prepare yourself as to what you need and what you don't need for your journey. Third, it empowers you to see beyond your weaknesses, falls, and mistakes. Last, it makes it easier for you to explain it clearly to those who matter in the cause.

Understanding the Principle of Planning

This is another essential principle every good leader must cultivate. The best way to properly manage time and change is to plan. Planning is simply putting time into your vision and systematically mapping out an outline or a pathway to your end goal. Just like a builder, you always need to have a plan that will systematically show how you are going to put up the building. The plan will show you the cost, the materials, the number of workers needed, and the estimated time of completion. Planning maps out your whole vision on paper. In the book of Habakkuk 2:2, God instructed the prophet to translate his vision into a plan and make it plain, which also means make it simple and easy to understand as well as known to all, so whenever the people see the plan, they will work toward its achievement: "And the Lord answered me, and said, write the vision, and make it plain upon tables, that he may run that readeth it."

Planning, which is applying time to purpose, does not tell you only what to do but also what you don't have to do. For example, if you plan to travel from A to B, your GPS (which contains your plan) will tell you which exits to take and which exits to avoid to not prolong your journey unnecessarily.

Planning also gives you the opportunity to split the vision into sections, called goals, and this makes you know what to do daily in the pursuit of the vision. Planning puts you to work so you don't waste precious time unnecessarily, as in Habakkuk, so that anyone who sees the plan will run in fulfillment of the vision, because a plan will always give you the motivation to run. A vision remains in the abstract if it's still a vision but becomes tangible when translated into a plan, and then it also gives you the motivation to work.

There is a saying that if you fail to plan, you are planning to fail, because planning gives you purpose for life. If you don't have a plan for your life, you wake up every morning with no sense of purpose or direction. Planning also gives you hope for the future. You might be in a messy situation now, but planning inspires you to know that your situation is temporary because you have planned your way out.

"And he said, come. And when Peter was come down out of the ship, he walked on the water, to go to Jesus. But when he saw the wind boisterous, he was afraid; and beginning to sink, he cried, saying, Lord, save me" (Matt. 14:29–30). In this passage, Peter asked Jesus to let him walk on the sea to Him, and so Jesus asked him to come, and as Peter stepped out of the ship, his focus was on Jesus, his destination, or in other words, his vision. So as long as Peter kept his focus on the vision, he was OK, but the moment he was distracted from his vision, he began to sink.

In life there are so many distractions, especially the moment you decide to pursue your purpose. Sometimes your very family or friends will distract you because you cannot do the same things you used to do with them. Some of the distractions may come in the form of lack of funds, or disappointments in relationships, or lack of higher education, but in all this, what can keep you going is keeping your focus on your vision.

Focus simply means constantly keeping your mind on your destination, and your focus will always produce determination, and determination is the fuel for success. You can never be determined if you don't constantly have your destination on your mind.

Focus also produces hope. If you are focused, no matter how much of the boisterous winds blow around you, no matter how much of the hardships you endure, you always have hope that come what may, you will work your way to your destination.

Focus produces discipline that will always keep you in check to always follow the plan. Lack of focus is one major reason why most people make resolution after resolution and then never fulfill them.

Understanding the Principle of Commitment

Commitment is the act of discipline to follow through to the very end with a promise or a decision. Commitment is your loyalty or devotion to a cause, and this is vital to leadership and a successful life. Commitment is seen when it is not convenient; when it is convenient, that is not commitment because anyone could do it. Anybody could have a vision, but what makes you successful is when you are committed to the cause and endure the highs and the lows with a positive attitude. Commitment is the heart to pursue the cause no matter what the price is, and it also preserves your integrity as a leader.

Recently, I read a story about a father who was committed to his word, so much so that his son took his promise as the gospel. One morning he dropped off his seven-year-old son at school, and after kissing him good-bye, he told him, "I will pick you up after school." About an hour to the school's closing time, the father heard on the news that there had been an earthquake in the area of his son's school. He quickly set off to the school, which was about an hour's drive, and upon arrival the father saw that the whole school building was in shambles. The police and the paramedics were busily working, pulling out dead bodies, and people in the neighborhood were crying in despair. The father made his way through the crowd of wailing parents and sympathizers toward where he perceived to be his child's classroom. He started removing brick after brick of debris and beams out of his way, even when he was told by the crowd of spectators not to bother because no child could have survived such mayhem. He chose to ignore the people and their pleas to go home and just accept the fact that he'd lost a son.

He kept removing debris and beams out of his way until the early hours of the next morning, when he heard what sounded like groaning, so he kept moving stuff out of his way with his bare hands. Finally, he was able to see a leg of a child, so he managed to get the debris off him and realized the child was alive. He continued digging stuff out of his way till he got to his son, who was also alive. He managed to save the whole class of about sixteen children; by the time he was done, it was noon the following day. At the hospital, his son's teacher, who was also saved, said that immediately after the earthquake occurred, his son kept assuring the class that his father would come get them, and lo and behold, he came to get them. Due to one man's commitment to his word, a whole class left to perish was saved.

Responsibility is one powerful word, and if understood correctly, it will totally transform your thinking and your attitude. Responsibility means you have the ability to respond; therefore, whatever has been entrusted into your care, you have the ability to deliver. Whenever something goes wrong with what has been entrusted to you, responsibility applies in two ways: you did not respond according to your ability and you are going to respond according to your ability to fix it. So you don't get off the hook.

Responsibility produces accountability, so if you feel responsible, you will feel accountable, and because you feel accountable, you will act according to your ability, or in other words, according to the expectations of your ability. Responsibility also produces action; whenever you feel responsible, you will go to work, you will act, and you will act right because you know you will be accountable. Responsibility is an attribute of one who is determined to make an influence in his or her community. To be a successful leader, you must cultivate the principle of responsibility, for if you are responsible, you take initiative and take charge of your environment. If you realize that your leadership responsibility is to serve humanity, it edges you to be looking for opportunities to serve.

Probity should not be the motivation for accountability for a leader; responsibility should be. The moment probity becomes the foundation for accountability, it utters the foundation of truth for responsibility. In other words, if you can cover up your tracks to pass probity, then you no longer feel responsible to be accountable. Accountability based on responsibility makes the positive effect on community a priority and not a personality. This means that if your actions or inactions will not affect the community positively, then you have to rethink it because you are first accountable to your purpose. This is where integrity comes in, and the moment probity becomes the basis for accountability, it becomes egoistic, then you become accountable to your ambitions, and ambitions serve you and not the community.

Sometimes people use probity as the basis for responsibility to avoid making a mistake, because they want to be seen as perfect leaders (a sure sign of ambition). The world doesn't need perfect leaders; the world needs leaders who will do the right thing.

If Thomas Edison were scared of making a mistake in making the first lightbulb because of probity, he wouldn't have done it. Because in the cause of probing, it would come to light that he made a thousand mistakes in his attempt to do the right thing, and that would tarnish his image. Instead, he knew that he was accountable to his purpose, which was to serve his community, so he cared less about the mistakes he was going to make in his pursuit to fulfill his purpose.

8

Africa's Crises of Corruption and Aid

For centuries now scholars and patriots of the continent have researched and dissected Africa's problems of poverty and corruption, and many solutions have been prescribed. Some of the prescriptions have helped in the short term, to some extent, but still the progress of the continent is unusually slow.

Corruption is the fruit of poor administrative management and a lack of purposeful leadership. Corruption is due to misinformation, which leads to misconception, where money is celebrated and service is demeaned. Enacting punitive laws against corruption is ineffective without investing resources into correctly educating the people to create the right perception of life and create in them leadership character.

Some of the prescriptions have suggested changes in the governing system from mostly military governance to democratic governance, which was seen by some as foreign, but reluctantly that wind of change is gradually but slowly gaining roots in Africa.

There have been numerous international programs to assist in the development of Africa to provide a better life for its people. In 2000, for instance, the African Growth and Opportunity Act (AGOA) was signed into law by President Bill Clinton to help improve Africa's economy.

Also, in 1996, the International Monetary Fund launched Highly Indebted Poor Countries (HIPC) to grant about $76.9 billion in debt relief to about thirty-six countries, of which thirty are African countries, and was projected to reduce debt stock by 90 percent.[1]

Others include the following:

- United States Development Assistance to Africa, under the United States Agency for International Development (USAID)
- United Nations' Millennium Development Goal (MDG), which was set up to assist with primary education under the Fast Track Initiative (FTI)
- Canadian Foreign Aid under Canadian International Development Agency (CIDA)
- Forum on China-Africa Cooperation (FOCAC)
- India-Africa Business Forum
- Tokyo International Conference of African Development (TICAD)

---

1 See http://www.imf.org/en/About/Factsheets/Sheets/2016/08/01/16/11/Debt-Relief-Under-the-Heavily-Indebted-Poor-Countries-Initiative.

We can go on and on about all these programs set up by all the other continents of the world to invest into Africa's development, but can we confidently say that all the billions of dollars pumped into Africa has been used judiciously for its development? Has all this aid flowing into Africa helped build up or plunder the continent?

Africans are people who once thought of themselves as warriors and builders of powerful kingdoms of rulership, but when they came into contact with the Western world, they were conquered, subdued, and then reduced to the level of a beast of the field. How did that happen?

On January 20, 1832, in the Virginia House of Delegates, Senator Henry Berry made this statement in the house: "We have, as far as possible, closed every avenue by which light might enter [the slaves'] minds. We have only to go one step further, to extinguish their capacity to see the light, and our work will be completed. They would then be reduced to the level of the beasts of the field, and we should be safe."

The only entity that has the ability to rule over another entity is that which has the power to reason and to plan. That is why man was made a ruler over the animals on earth, and it's the same reason why man can tame the wildest animal on earth. So, to rule over another person, you have to bring him or her to the level of the beast of the field.

Even though this statement was made in the United States, it gives me an idea how the West was seeing Africa. This suggests to me that a systematic approach was taken to make sure that Africa was broken so the Western world should feel safe. As we just established, you cannot rule over another ruler until you bring him to the level of the beast of the field, and that was what was done to Africa. Africans were made to believe that they were less of a human, robbed of their confidence and self-worth, and convinced of the lie that they were cursed as descendants of Canaan. "And he said, cursed be Canaan; a servant of servants shall he be unto his brethren" (Gen. 9:25). In this curse that Noah pronounced on his grandchild, it did not transcend unto generations; Noah cursed Canaan and Canaan alone. If you look throughout scriptures, a curse has to be pronounced generationally before it can affect the descendant, but this particular curse never mentioned generations and never mentioned descendants, period. The concept that Africa was cursed to serve the West is a blatant lie.

Africa was brainwashed to believe that the Caucasian is next to God, if not God himself, and this belief influenced Africans' perception of dependence on the West. This belief even influenced a popular adage in the Akan culture in Ghana that says, "When you are on your way to church and you meet a white man, you have to go back home because you've met God." In other words, you were going to church to be in fellowship with God, so if you meet Him on your way, there is no need to go waste your time in church because you've already met God.

This explains why some Africans willingly or reluctantly participated in the slave trade—many did it out of coercion, but some did it because they thought they were doing it for God.

Then again, when the Western world first came into contact with Africa around the 1420s, Africa was at a very critical and important point in its stage of development. It was the period of wars by the kingdoms to determine their boundaries that would have resulted in fewer countries on the continent as well as fewer languages spoken, especially sub-Saharan Africa.

If the Western world had not interrupted Africa's process, the most powerful kingdoms would have conquered the least ones, which would have resulted in fewer kingdoms of rulership, which later would have been countries. This would have also assimilated the smaller tribes into the bigger ones, which would have also resulted in fewer languages.

If you take a look at the artificial boundaries set by the Western world in Africa, this came with its own problems of creating too many countries. Then again, some tribes were split into two countries—for instance, Ewes in the Volta region of Ghana were split between Ghana and Togo, and the Nzima were also split between Ghana and Ivory Coast.

All these backdrops contributed greatly to Africa's current crisis, but they are not excuses for Africa not rising. You see, we can blame the Western world for Africa's setback, but it is Africa's sole responsibility to rise. And if you have an understanding of historical factors contributing to a problem, it puts you in a better position to know how to tackle it. As my grandma always says, "You can blame someone for pushing you down, but you have to blame yourself for not getting up."

Against these backgrounds, coupled with the kingdom structure of rulership whose motivation is power, profit, and ownership, Africans' perspective of leadership is influencing their attitude now. Looking at the crisis in Africa now, one can easily link it to their historic experience of kingdoms of rulership and slavery, which resulted in their broken image and reinforced their concept of corporate leadership that is deeply entrenched in the politicosociocultural fiber of their society.

So no matter how much money is pumped into Africa, or how many programs are designed for them by the international community, or how many changes of government are endured, if the African mind-set is not changed, the cycle will continue from generation to generation. The problem with Africa is that the people have bought and engrained in their subconscious the concept of corporate leadership, whose motivation is money, power, and control. As we discussed earlier, corporate leadership can easily become a weapon of destruction. So having elections is just an aspect of democracy, but understanding the structures or the pillars of democracy is a whole different ball game. You ought to have the attitude of service leadership to understand the whole structure of democracy.

Take a look at a few of these African heads of state, and you will see the exhibition of corporate leadership traits—wherein they feel they made the countries, so they own the countries:

- Teodoro Obiang Nguema Mbasogo, who has been the president of Equatorial Guinea for about thirty-seven years
- Jose Eduardo Dos Santos, president of Angola for thirty-seven years
- Paul Biya, who has ruled over the people of Cameroon for about thirty-four years
- Yoweri Museveni, who has ruled over the people of Uganda for about thirty years

Really, we cannot blame them because they are a product of their societies and will always argue that democracy is not for Africa. But that is because they have believed in the wrong concept of leadership, which gives them a wrong perspective, making them act wrongly. The problem is that Africa has bought into the concept of rulership so much so that its leaders feel they are doing their nations a favor. I am using the word "wrong" not because corporate leadership is wrong, but it's being applied in the wrong context. If you ask most Africans what their definition of leadership is, you definitely will hear about power, wealth, control, authority, and so on. So, with this concept, people aspire to leadership just to fulfill their cynical ambitions.

All of the programs and projects in Africa are targeting the stem of its problems and not the roots, which is the mind-set of the people, and until we change the mind-set of the African, we will have the whole world doing community service in Africa and nothing will change.

The reason most people misbehave, especially African administrative officeholders, is the lack of understanding of leadership. Most of these people think that leadership is an office or power, so it makes them arrogant, but if they know that it is a gift for service and that everybody has it, they will see their role as an opportunity for service and not a privilege to rule.

We also need to examine the issue of aid to Africa. Is it because the Western world feels guilty about plundering Africa? Is it a system to keep Africa dependent on the West? Or is it a smoke screen behind which the Western world is hiding to keep Africa in its turmoil to remain a reservoir of wealth to feed their status? Or it is out of genuine hearts to help Africa?

Well, whatever the answer is, it is also a fact that aid efforts are not helping Africa, especially the ones going to African governments. Most of the aid goes to line the pockets of the politicians and makes them wealthy and powerful to manipulate and bully the people the more, and the money does not get to the people. Most African politicians come to power poor, and, in no time, they become wealthy.

Besides the fact that it breeds corruption, aid also stifles initiative and creativity on the part of the government recipients. As the saying goes, "Give a fish to the hungry, and he will always come to you for fish, but teach the hungry to fish, and he will never come to you for fish." Because these rulers know they can have access to easy money, they don't think outside the box to develop creative programs to help create wealth for their people. It also does not encourage accountability but rather reckless monetary spending on the part of the African governments.

The aid to Africa creates dependency on the West by the African recipients, and dependency stifles initiative and induces coercion and a level of control, not just over the people but also over their resources. Therefore, the aid to Africa makes the independence of Africa quasi independence.

Aid gets African heads of state off the hook of accountability because without the aid, they may be forced to provide the road they use to solicit for votes, and if they are unable to provide the road, then the electorates will vote against them. Since they want to win elections, they will then be forced to sit up and think of ways to develop resources internally, both human and capital, to keep power.

About a trillion dollars has been pumped into Africa for the past fifty to sixty years, and Africa is still wallowing in poverty. Government aid has outlived its usefulness. Aid to Africa was supposed to serve as savings for the newly independent countries that needed money as savings to invest to achieve growth. Now that it's been over fifty years, the question is, does Africa still needs savings?

In my opinion, if aid is needed at all, it should be channeled to the credible NGOs that are on the ground working hard to create a better life for the people.

Recently my seven-year-old son picked up one of his belts and read the inscription on the tag, "Made in China," and the next questions he asked were, "Dad, why was the belt made in China? Does it mean we cannot do it?" I had to take my time to explain to him the free-market economy and also let him know that importing goods from a different country does not mean people in that country are better than us. This is where we don't see the harm it causes the younger generation because it took time for me to convince him that it has nothing to do with our ability to manufacture goods as a nation. Recently, I also heard in the news that Nigeria is importing *gari*, locally made cassava flakes that are very common to most West Africans. *Gari*, which I believe most typical Nigerian children, especially those raised in the rural areas, would know how to prepare, should never be imported to a country like Nigeria.

Come to think of it, first of all, you are using the hard-earned dollars to import a commodity that could serve as an income industry for the deprived areas of Nigeria. Assuming *gari* is in high demand, and production is not meeting the demands, this should be an industrial venture for the locals. All you need to do is mobilize the local rural youth and set up *gari*-producing factories, which could serve as an income venture for the youth as well as meeting the *gari* demands of the nation and, if possible, export to the neighboring African countries.

The negative psychological effects on the younger generation of some of these imported goods are so damaging that we may not even know the extent of it. It destroys their pride and confidence in the ability and potentials of the nation, and it also stifles the initiative of the youth.

The wealthiest and most powerful place on earth is not the gold-mining fields of South Africa, or the oil fields in the Gulf, or the diamond-mining fields in Russia, but the mining fields of the human brain. Until Africa realizes this truth and invests in the mining fields of the African brains, with all its natural resources, the continent will continue to wallow in poverty. If Africa invests into the mining fields of its brains, it will experience the ultimate benefits of its natural resource.

Now, the most essential and yet difficult part in solving Africa's crisis is the changing of the mentality of the people. One cannot change a concept that has been entrenched in the culture of people for centuries in a few years; it needs a systematic and a methodological approach. One thing we have to understand is that we can inspire and motivate the people all we want, inspire them to see the new paradigm of leadership, but motivation and inspiration will wear out. Rather, we need to change their mind-sets and their thought processes by the only way to introduce a true transformation, as it is recorded in Romans 12:2: "And be not conformed to this world: but be ye transformed by the renewing of your mind, that ye may prove what is that good, and acceptable, and perfect, will of God."

In other words, we don't have to conform to the system, and the only way we can change our circumstances is by renewing the mind. Inspiration and motivation alone would not work. But in addition, there has to be a systematic program to renew the mind, so that change will come from within. No amount of prayer can transform the situation; the only way transformation can take place is by having a new mind-set, by thinking out of the system. When your mind is changed, you don't need motivation and inspiration; as a matter of fact, you become the motivation and the inspiration. Change comes from the mind-set, not from the emotions, where inspiration and motivation comes from.

For Africa to start seeing some real progress, there has to be a vigorous attempt to change the thinking process of the young people. In view of this, primary education is essential, and this bedrock of human education must be free and mandatory for all youth. Primary education needs a critical look; it needs to be fine-tuned to develop the thinking faculty of the younger generation.

Introduction of Critical Thinking

Critical thinking simply means asking the three basic questions all the time: *Why* is something the way it is? *How* do I solve a problem to fulfill the purpose of the problem? And *what* will be the effect? Your ability to reason influences your choices: If you reason right, you will make right choices, and if you reason wrongly, you will make wrong choices. Therefore, critical thinking is vital to living a successful leadership life. Africa needs to shift its emphasis from authority to critical thinking because critical thinkers will always appreciate the right authority. Currently, African's value authority seems to be gaging critical thinking.

A systematic approach has to go into preparing the younger generation for service leadership in the future. One of the first areas that needs to be looked at is the educational curriculum of African schools, starting from primary education to tertiary education. It needs a total overhaul of uneducating and reeducating the youth right from kindergarten throughout higher-learning institutions.

Critical thinking programs and subjects need to be introduced to primary education. Critical thinking is one of the essential components lacking in the African educational programs, which affects the youth in analyzing issues when confronted with them. Critical thinking is essential in the development of the human society, especially in these days when the world is running at a very fast rate. Success in life depends on how critical one can think through problems. The world is now in the era of information development; ideas are valuable and powerful. Nations are now being built on ideas, relegating natural resources to the back seat.

It is amazing how the colonial masters of Africa designed Africa's educational system to benefit the Western world, and yet after independence, Africans did nothing to develop an educational system to reflect their uniquenesses. African schools still read books about African history written by Western authors. Africans need to invest in rebuilding their schools by taking ownership of their educational systems. Africans can forget about being a force to reckon with if they refuse to take ownership of their educational systems.

As a matter of fact, there are nations with very limited natural resources that have been able to progress by investing in the development of their human resources. America has natural resources, but that is not what is making it great. Americans invested and are still investing in the human resources of the future. As a matter of fact, America is reserving most of its natural resources for future generations. The most important resources needed for nation building is not natural resources but human resources. The human brain is the only resource you need for nation building; any other resource is a bonus.

For people to think critically or positively, they must first value themselves to know that they are capable of thinking through any problem they face. Successful people always know their value, as the psalmist said in Psalm 139:14, "I will praise thee; for I am fearfully and wonderfully made: marvelous are thy works; and that my soul knoweth right well." Self-worth is what sets successful people apart, and if that can be taught to the young ones, no barrier can stand in their way. Self-worth also makes one discover himself or herself, so at an early age, if the young ones discover themselves, it sets them up for success. It also produces self-confidence, which is lacking in the African society to the point that it is confused with arrogance. There is an enormous power in self-worth; it makes you feel like you own the entire world.

Introduction of Patriotism and Nationalism

This is another virtue that is missing in the African society, and lack of patriotism and nationalism produces corruption. It is also the cause of injustice that breeds distrust of officials, resulting in instant justice, a very brutal and barbaric act that is rampant in African society. Patriotism and nationalism are very powerful attributes that exhume love and respect not only for one's country but also for humanity. It has to start by instilling into the young ones the pledge of allegiance, and this will produce a sense of belonging and service to the nation.

The young ones need to be made the vision carriers; in other words, the vision of the country or the continent needs to be properly documented and inculcated in their school curriculum. The vision also needs to be made available to all and abridged especially for the young ones, and it needs to be ingrained in every fiber of their being so they can grow with it. This will help guide their choices and instill in them a sense of determination and dedication for nation building. Investing in the reeducation of the youth is vital since that is the only way to set Africa on the right path to raising a new breed of leadership that understands service to humanity.

Introduction of Service Leadership

The introduction of service leadership in the primary school curriculum is the key to unlocking Africa's hidden beautiful future to the world. If you look at great and powerful nations, they were built on mostly service leadership, with a fraction of corporate leadership. The African setup is the opposite; the nations are being built on mostly corporate leadership and a negligible fraction on service leadership.

Africa is confused due to disappointments and misinformation about leadership, which leads to Africa losing its identity in the world today. Leadership has been misconstrued, misrepresented, and misinterpreted to the demise of Africa and to the advantage of Western society. Now we have come to understand that leadership is not what has been written in the books.

What's in the books is what the Western world has cooked up to create the system for Africans to be where we are, to be controlled and manipulated, and for Westerners to take advantage of us. They make us understand that leadership is about power, so all we do is to pursue power to be counted or to be respected. They tell us that leadership is about position, so we do anything to get positions. They tell us leadership is about amassing or influencing followers, so that is what we pursue, and when we are not able to attain all that, we become disappointed and confused because we have been misinformed. This will then give the designers of the system the opportunity to exploit us to their advantage, and we will be running around in circles in our confusion, killing and destroying one another in our pursuit of all the power, the position, the influence, and all that they claim leadership is. We tend to be like other people; we tend to copy from too many nations that we lose our identity and become a laughingstock in the world. We need to rediscover our own unique identity to earn the dignity and respect we deserve in our world.

Life has been described and defined by many people based on their experiences, so if you happen to be rich, your description will be on the basis of your experiences of the joy your money has been able to afford you. If you are poor, it will be based on the experiences of lack in your life, and if you live in a war zone or an unjust environment, it will be defined by the pain and the agony of your experience. People's definitions of life vary because their experiences vary. Some will say life is fun because they are having fun moments like partying, vacations, and so forth. Others will say life is too short because they have lost some young loved one. No matter what our definitions are based on our experiences, however, it does not change God's purpose and definition of life. God would never be fair if He created life only to be defined by our experiences—and then the statement "life is not fair" would hold—but God is much wiser than that.

If you read the book of Ecclesiastes, especially the first two chapters, you will see that one of the wisest kings ever lived on the planet Earth. He was endowed with wisdom from God, and he gave his heart to wisdom and understanding, which are supposed to be the keys to life's success, and yet he struggled to find the meaning of life. For a king like Solomon, you would think that the meaning of life should come to him without a struggle, but reading the early chapters of Ecclesiastes, you will realize that ambition took a better part of him during the prime of his life. "And whatsoever mine eyes desired I kept not from them, I withheld not my heart from any joy; for my heart rejoiced in all my labour: and this was my portion of all my labour. Then I looked on all the works that my hands had wrought, and on the labour that I had laboured to do: and behold: all was vanity and vexation of spirit, and there was no profit under the sun" (Eccles. 2:10–11). Compare his statements here to that of his father in Psalm 8:5–6: "For thou hast made him a little lower than the angels, and hast crowned him with glory and honour. Thou madest him to have dominion over the works of thy hands; thou hast put all things under his feet." Here King David was celebrating the lives of men who lived their lives in the purpose of God.

Any time you live outside of God's purpose for your life, you will struggle with the meaning and fulfillment in life. Life is not meant to be a struggle; pursue wisdom and understanding and find your purpose to serve your generation, and life will be fulfilling and meaningful to you. When you fulfill your purpose, remember, you are preparing the next generation to fulfill their part as well.

There are two, and only two, reasons the world is in turmoil, especially in Africa: (1) because man is busy trying to play God in the area of rulership over another man, which he can never be, and (2) because man is not being like God in the area of purpose and creativity in the rulership over the earth to be the leader he was created to be.

9

Conclusion: An Ode to a Leader Unknown to the World

I want to salute and celebrate one of the greatest leaders the world has ever known in the history of humanity. He was a man who dedicated his entire life to the service of humanity and did what he was born to do to change the world. He was leadership personified, and it can be said of him without a shadow of doubt that he served his generation and can now rest with his fathers. He is no other person than Dr. David Fuseini Abdulai.

Dr. Abdulai, as he was popularly called, or the "Mad Doctor," was one of a kind; he was a man who knew who he was and what his assignment on earth was. He was a man who defied all excuses in life, and his testament gives credence to the fact that life is not about what you have but what you do with what you have.

Dr. Abdulai was the founder of the Shekhina Clinics at Gurugu (since 1989) and Wamale, both in the northern region of Ghana, West Africa. He was born to a very poor family in the northern region of Ghana. His father suffered from leprosy and died while Dr. Abdulai was still a young man, about twenty-three years old. He became the only survivor of eleven children. His mother, who was a beggar, was so dear to him, and he was by her deathbed in 1999.

He was born on December 18, 1951, even though he was not too sure of the date because his parents were uneducated and couldn't document his date of birth. According to him, he chose this date based on events told to him surrounding his birth, which alluded to the conviction that he was born around, if not on, this date.

When he was a young boy, Dr. Abdulai came into contact with some Irish Catholic missionaries who put him through elementary school with the permission of his parents. Even though he was born into a family that practiced the traditional faith (they even kept a shrine in the house where his dad performed traditional rituals), his religious inclinations didn't matter to his family. According to Dr. Abdulai, his father was a free-spirited man who was always happy and would always tell his son that God loves him so much that He would never disappoint him, and Dr. Abdulai should always keep his trust in God, and this became his crutch to lean on when the going got tough.

He was an exceptionally brilliant student, but due to financial hardships, he became a street boy for a while. He was very athletic and loved entertainment in school, and between 1966 and 1973, while he was in Tamale Secondary

School, he became a house prefect. He also became a Muslim in secondary school for three years. Most of his schooling was done with benevolence, especially by the Catholic missionary. After completing secondary school successfully, he was enrolled in the University of Ghana, where he chose to study medicine.

While in the university, he became a free thinker for three years, until one day he went to see the university Catholic chaplain to discuss his confusion on religion and to seek counsel. To his surprise, the father didn't make any attempt to convert him to Catholicism, but rather he told him that if he couldn't be a Christian, he should be a Muslim because it is not good to not belong to any religion. The fact that the father didn't force Christianity on him moved him so much that he decided to become a Christian because he realized that Christianity would give him the fulfillment he needed in his life.

In the university he failed his supposed best subject, math, in the first-year university exams. This demoralized him for a moment, but he quickly learned a lesson out of that failure. He said in an interview that from that moment, his eyes were opened to a life of truth, and he stopped his ambitions of wanting to be at the top and decided to find the real meaning of happiness in life. He went on to become a medical doctor in 1979.

After he graduated with honors from the University of Ghana, he won a fellowship to do a postgraduate study in tropical medicine at Liverpool School of Medicine. He also went to Zambia to do a two-year study in surgery and then returned to Ghana to practice in the capital city Accra. He lived in Accra with his wife, Doris, and his children for a while before he decided to embark on his life's purpose to serve the poor, sick, and destitute in the northern region of Ghana. His marriage to Doris ended after twenty-four years, and he eventually remarried.

This was a man whose doom was spelled out right from his birth, but due to determination, perseverance, and hard work, he discovered his leadership seed. Knowing that he had an assignment to fulfill and that the world would never be the same with or without him, he pressed on and stepped over every hurdle that stood in his way to get to the finish line.

He invested his life savings into building the first of the two Shekhinah Clinics to provide free medical care to the poor, sick, and destitute in the city of Tamale in March 1991. According to him, he developed the act of giving from his beloved mother, who even on her deathbed was still giving out her life's meager possessions—what an amazing woman. His wonderful mother gave away all of her belongings and was left with only the clothes on her back, in which she died.

The Shekhinah Clinic became a home to the homeless and treated the sick, fed the poor, and sheltered the displaced free of charge. Dr. Abdulai assembled a team of twenty-seven medical professionals who also sacrificed their lives working at the Shekhinah Clinics without being paid. These were people who were truly dedicated to the service of humanity. They could have made a fortune working in prestigious hospitals in Ghana since the medical profession is one of the fortune-making industries in Ghana. These young medical professionals understood Dr. Abdulai's vision, however, and bought into it to become channels of blessing to their generation.

Dr. Abdulai was nicknamed the "Mad Doctor" because of his affection for humanity and dedication to the mentally challenged and those who had been neglected by society, and he reached out to them and extended a hand of love to them. The two clinics saw about 120 patients a day, and on January 6, 1992, he instituted a daily-feeding program, in which about 150 of the sick, hungry, destitute, and vulnerable were fed every day until now. In 1989, he started his annual Christmas party, in which about three thousand strangers are entertained with food, drinks, music, and fellowship, and this has been going on annually until now. According to him, all of this he did by divine providence and donations from individuals, companies, and charity organizations such as USAID, Catholic Relief Services, and the United Nations World Food Program.

In 2008 the embassy of the United States in Ghana instituted the Martin Luther King Jr. Award for peace and social justice to recognize, appreciate, and honor Ghanaian personalities who are contributing to the development of humanities based on the concepts and philosophies of Dr. King. In 2012 Dr. Abdulai became the fifth recipient of this award.

It is surprising that the world is not blowing the trumpets of celebration over the life of such an angelic being who lived among men on earth. This was a man who personified love in action and ought to be celebrated by humanity. If possible, we should make him a saint, as was done for Mother Teresa, since he was also a Catholic. This man was indeed an angel loaned to the world. In May 2016, he was diagnosed with stage-four thyroid cancer, and on October 2, 2016, at the age of sixty-five, he gave up the ghost to go be with the Lord.

He left behind a wife and three children.

At the end of the day, when the dust settles and the sun is resting, we may not all know who you were, and we may not all celebrate you, but the people you were born to serve will know that you once lived a life worthy of a crown.

It is my prayer that this book will transform a life and give meaning and purpose to someone who was heading down the path of hopelessness, disappointment, and destruction. I also pray that it will set Africa at liberty from its shackles of mental bondage, poverty, and illiteracy and put it on the path to self-discovery, self-worth, prosperity, and raising a new breed of leaders who will understand the true values of leadership to serve the continent selflessly and passionately with pride and transform the continent to what God intended it to be. The greatest leader, is one who acknowledges the rulership of God over humanity.

Your leadership service defines your value to humanity, and remember that leadership is not obtained but rather attained.

Amen.

References

http://www.worldbank.org/en/topic/debt/brief/hipc

Published in October 10, 2016 by The World Bank under heavily indebted poor country (HIPC) initiative "David Abdulai." *Wikipedia*. https://en.wikipedia.org/wiki/David_Abdulai.

Lago, Leslie Pastén. "Touching Lives—Dr. David Abdulai," 2012. https://www.youtube.com/watch?v=6opHLxSGTUI.

Mandela, Nelson. "I Am Prepared to Die." Speech given at the Rivonia Trial in South Africa, April 20, 1964. https://en.wikipedia.org/wiki/I_Am_Prepared_to_Die-.

———. *Long Walk to Freedom: The Autobiography of Nelson Mandela*. Little Brown & Co., 1994.

MyJoyOnline TV. "Personality Profile—PM Express," 2012. https://www.youtube.com/watch?v=tGzsjxt5khA.